How to Be a History Geek

500 Addictive History Trivia and Fun Facts for Smart Kids and Curious Adults

Bryan Mack

Table of Contents

Introduction

A good knowledge of history is a quiver full of arrows in debates.

–Winston Churchill

When trivia is done right, it's anything but trivial. It can be a fun family evening or a night with friends, making connections and discovering new interests. It can be a cognitive exercise, working the memory and flexing the mental muscles for entertainment and improvement. It's *always* an adventure in curiosity, of discovering who humans are now and who we have been and how the latter informed the former.

Each of these 500 questions is a call to action, a gateway to a world of intrigue, innovation, and introspection that anyone can walk through. You can think of them as rabbit holes to go down, much like the modern social media YouTube rabbit hole, but these all lead to rich histories, interesting personalities, and world-shaking events. We'll start out in ancient times, touching briefly on prehistory before launching into written records of the first great human civilizations. We'll discuss how they interacted with one another culturally and politically and what changes that brought. We'll talk about innovations in politics, society, art, and even that deadliest of human inventions, warfare.

There are many ways to use this book, depending on your company.

- If you're looking for inspiration for something new to learn or read, you might flip open a chapter that interests you and read through, waiting for the question that catches your imagination.
- If you're on a long road trip, train ride, or flight, bring out the book and challenge your friends and family to see who can get the most questions right without missing one.
- If you're looking to become an expert on a certain topic, check out the questions in its chapter and use that as a jumping-off point.
- If you're in a classroom setting and looking for something to engage your students, try using these questions as a game to tickle their brains and get them interested.

- If you're a teacher, let students choose questions as a jumping off point for essays, presentations, projects, and group or independent studies.
- If you have downtime and need to occupy your mind, choose a chapter and read straight through, seeing how many you get right and how many you want to know more about.
- Choose a question as a conversation piece for family dinner times to keep everyone engaged and away from their screens for a while.
- Trade questions with fellow history fans and friends alike as a way to get to know their interests and level of history geekdom.

Hopefully, these 10 chapters cover a wide enough range of topics to make a history geek of anyone. History is much wilder and weirder than anything we could make up, and I hope this book proves that. If you enjoy this trivia and the gateways to history it pops open, please leave a review and share it with a friend. Maybe they'll walk through a gateway or two with you!

Chapter 1:

Giants of the Classical Word: Egypt, Greece, and Rome

When we talk about the Classical World or Classical Antiquity, we're talking about the civilizations that sprung up around the Mediterranean from about 1000 B.C. to 400 in the Common Era. These civilizations and their ever-changing connections to each other have had an outsized impact on the rest of human history in the West, where classical education is still revered to this day. Classical scholars, priests, rulers, and artists left copious written records—although it's always important to remember the bias of the writer in delivering history, just as it is when reading today's news.

Greece was the first of these civilizations to give way, but Egypt had the most incredible staying power—it changed hands and capitals and even religions but remained Egypt to the last. The struggle between Rome and Egypt, which ended with Caesar Augustus, Rome's first emperor, triumphant, had a truly outsized effect on the subsequent history of the world. As it was, Augustus won supreme control of the Empire, ruling from Rome itself, rather than the center of power shifting east to Alexandria, Cleopatra, and Antony. The Western world could be very different, had that struggle or even one of its many battles gone differently.

Because of its importance, the idea of the Classical World is often extended to the societies that existed before it—though in many cases those societies left no written records. We'll delve into those here as we explore in turn ancient Egypt, Greece, and Rome.

Questions

1. Ancient Egyptians loved board games, especially one called…
    a. Parcheesi
    b. Senet
    c. Seven Wonders
    d. Monopoly
2. In Ancient Egypt, pyramids were usually built by…
    a. Paid laborers
    b. Field hands
    c. Slaves
    d. Prisoners
3. In Ancient Egyptian hieroglyphics, some symbols represent ideas or concepts, while others represent…
    a. Other languages
    b. Parts of speech
    c. Offerings
    d. Sounds in the Ancient Egyptian language
4. This Egyptian goddess was depicted at different times both as a large lioness and a small, domestic cat.
    a. Isis
    b. Athena
    c. Bastet
    d. Hathor
5. The English word "paper" derives from Ancient Egyptian…
    a. Papyrus
    b. Bamboo
    c. Papillion
    d. Bes
6. Modern scholars couldn't read Ancient Egyptian hieroglyphics until after the discovery of…
    a. The Library of Alexandria
    b. Atlantis
    c. The Rosetta Stone
    d. The Code of Hammurabi
7. The Valley of the Kings is near the modern city of Luxor. When Egypt's rulers were building the valley's many grand tombs, Luxor was called…
    a. Cairo
    b. Thebes
    c. Marrakesh
    d. Giza
8. Ancient Egypt came under Roman rule after the death of this last pharaoh…
    a. Tutankhamun
    b. Cleopatra VII
    c. Hatshepsut
    d. Ramses II
9. Rulers of Ancient Egypt could predict how high the Nile river would flood each year using something called a…
    a. Nilometer
    b. River Raft
    c. Reed
    d. Censer

Answers

1. **B. Senet.** Since at least 3500 B.C., Ancient Egyptians played Senet, a game with a long board of 30 squares. We still don't know all the rules, but pharaohs were painted playing the game—and some were even buried with it! (Andrews, 2019).
2. **A. Paid laborers.** The pyramids were built mostly by paid laborers, many of whom were highly skilled craftspeople and artisans. While slaves were common in Egypt, the myth that they built the pyramids can be traced to Herodotus, who was writing in Greece nearly 2000 years after the fact (Andrews, 2019).
3. **D. Sounds in the Ancient Egyptian Language.** Hieroglyphs look like ideographs, or drawings of concepts they represent, and in many cases they are. However, other hieroglyphs represent sounds in Ancient Egyptian. This makes it a partly phonetic system of writing; the system you're using to read this book is entirely phonetic (Kiger, 2021).
4. **C. Bastet.** Cats of all sizes were beloved in Ancient Egypt. The goddess Bastet was at first depicted as an intimidating lioness. As her role in Ancient Egyptian religion changed throughout the centuries, she was later depicted as a domestic cat with a litter of kittens to protect (Yuko, 2021).
5. **A. Papyrus.** Papyrus is still made from the reeds of the papyrus plant, which grows in sunny, swampy areas like the Nile delta. While it's a specialty product today, Egyptian papyrus was the most popular writing material in the classical world (Szymanski, 2004).
6. **C. The Rosetta Stone.** In 196 B.C., Pharaoh Ptolemy V's government issued a decree chiseled in stone in three different languages and alphabets: Ancient Egyptian hieroglyphics, Demotic script, and Ancient Greek. The slab was rediscovered in 1799 by Napoleon's army, which led to 19th century scholars finally decoding the long-forgotten hieroglyphic writing system (Nix, 2018).
7. **B. Thebes.** During Egypt's New Kingdom (1550–1069 B.C.), many rulers built their tombs in the Valley across the river from the Ancient city of Thebes. The great temples of Luxor and Karnak were also in Thebes, which was the center of Egyptian religious life for millenia (Ministry of Antiquities, 2019).
8. **B. Cleopatra VII.** As then-mighty Rome was entering its Imperial era and gobbling up territory, Queen Cleopatra VII of Egypt skillfully kept Egypt's autonomy intact. Although her son technically became pharaoh after her suicide in the year 30 B.C., he was assassinated within weeks, and Egypt officially became part of the Roman Empire under Augustus.
9. **A. Nilometer.** Each year, the success and bounty of the Egyptian harvest was reliant on how high the Nile would rise, flooding its valley with rich, black soil in which to grow the year's crops. Egypt was the breadbasket of the ancient world, so the ability to predict the harvest was important for those in power (Atlas Obscura, 2017).

Questions

10. This Pharaoh came to power in the 1350s B.C. and started a temporary sea change in Ancient Egyptian religion, setting aside other gods and elevating the Aten.
    a. Khufu
    b. Thutmose III
    c. Nefertari
    d. Akhenaten
11. Of all the Seven Wonders of the Ancient World, this Egyptian one is the only one still standing.
    a. The Valley of the Kings
    b. Caesar's Palace
    c. The Great Pyramid of Giza
    d. The Lighthouse of Alexandria
12. When a mummy was created in Ancient Egypt, often the lungs, liver, stomach, and intestines were extracted and stored in…
    a. The Organ Cupboard
    b. Canopic Jars
    c. A Dutch Oven
    d. Ice
13. The oldest important stone building from Ancient Egypt that still exists is…
    a. The Step Pyramid at Saqqārah
    b. The Column of Ra
    c. The Temple of Artemis
    d. The Palace of Alexandria
14. In Ancient Egyptian cosmology, this animal was associated with the sun traveling across the sky and the idea of rebirth.
    a. Goat
    b. Sheep
    c. Cow
    d. Beetle
15. Ancient Greece was divided into city-states, a political and geographic region called a…
    a. Polis
    b. Agora
    c. Mediterranean
    d. Democracy
16. The famous Oracle of Delphi spoke her prophecies from a temple devoted to this Greek god.
    a. Zeus
    b. Poseidon
    c. Hella
    d. Apollo
17. *The Iliad* is Ancient Greek poet Homer's tale of the Trojan War, including the feats of Trojan warrior Hector and Greek warrior…
    a. Athena
    b. Achilles
    c. Alexander
    d. Aramis

Answers

10. **D. Akhenaten.** Pharaoh Amenhotep IV changed his name to Ahkenaten to reflect his changing religious ideas; he no longer worshiped Amun but focused on the Aten. He changed art, culture, religion, and moved his capital city to fit his view in the 17 years of his reign (Taronas, 2023).
11. **C. The Great Pyramid of Giza.** All of the other Seven Wonders of the Ancient World have been destroyed over time, including the other Egyptian one, the Lighthouse of Alexandria (National Geographic Society, 2022g).
12. **B. Canopic Jars.** These four jars are often carved with the head of their protector-deity, one of the four sons of the falcon-headed god Horus, god of the afterlife. Hapy protects the lungs, Duamutef protects the stomach, Imsety protects the liver, and Qebehsenuef protects the intestines (The Met, 2020).
13. **A. The Step Pyramid at Saqqārah.** Memphis was the capital by the 3rd Dynasty (c. 2650–c. 2575 B.C.), and its second king, Djoser, loved architectural innovation. He had the Step Pyramid built, laying the foundation for Egyptian royal tomb-building to come (Editors of Encyclopedia Britannica, 2015).
14. **D. Beetle.** The scarab beetle is known for collecting and rolling its favorite prize, a ball of dung, from its place of origin back to the beetle's burrow. Ancient Egyptians thought the dung ball served as an egg as well as a food source, but in fact female scarab beetles lay their eggs in the dung (Simon, 2014).
15. **A. Polis.** Athens, Sparta, Thebes, and Rhodes were all *poleis*—which is the plural for *polis*. Each polis ran itself according to its own political philosophy, though they all considered themselves Greek (National Geographic Society, 2022a).
16. **D. Apollo.** Apollo is recognized as the god of light and the sun, archery, healing, music, and of course, prophecy. The Pythia or priestess at Delphi was very likely hallucinating and entranced from inhaling ethylene gas from a natural vent beneath the temple. Ancient Greeks believed that the Pythia had been predicting important world events since the beginning of time (History.com Editors, 2018b).
17. **B. Achilles.** In The Illiad, the warrior Achilles is the son of King Peleus and a Nereid or sea-nymph named Thetis. According to legend, Thetis was so worried about her son that she dipped him in the River Styx to protect him—unfortunately, she was holding him by the heel, which remained unprotected. This is where we get the "Achilles heel," both the literal and figurative.

Questions

18. Although this Greek philosopher wrote nothing down himself, he was the original teacher of and inspiration for Plato, who's considered the father of Western philosophy.
    a. Socrates
    b. Diogenes
    c. Archimedes
    d. Horatio
19. These Ancient Greek Warriors were frontline infantry, each man equipped with bronze armor, a spear, a short sword, and the shield that they're named for.
    a. Lion Troops
    b. Hoplites
    c. Trojans
    d. Retiarius
20. According to Ancient Greek religion, twelve of the most powerful gods lived here.
    a. Athens
    b. Mt. Olympus
    c. The Mediterranean Sea
    d. Crete
21. The first recorded Olympic Games took place in Greece in…
    a. 1992
    b. 2 B.C.
    c. 1231
    d. 776 B.C.
22. Sparta and Athens, both powerful Greek city-states, went head-to-head in this long and complicated war in the 5th Century B.C.
    a. The Trojan War
    b. The Peloponnesian War
    c. The Ionian Revolt
    d. The Cycladic War
23. When this Greek city-state shed its former system of rule by aristocracy, it initiated the first European democracy or *demokratia.*
    a. Athens
    b. Corinth
    c. Sparta
    d. Thebes
24. Ancient Greeks of all ages loved games, especially ones using these implements similar to modern dice.
    a. Ax-throwing
    b. Knucklebones
    c. Tiddlywinks
    d. Rabbit's feet

Answers

18. **A. Socrates.** To this day, students of philosophy and education learn the Socratic Method of questioning a topic or position. Socrates lived from 469–399 B.C. but he's still teaching us how to think critically today. Socrates's powerful opinions on right and wrong often put him in the crosshairs of the Athenian government, which was growing increasingly tyrannical around that time. He was convicted of failing to honor the gods and corrupting the young. Eventually, and famously, he was forced to drink hemlock. It's said he went willingly, prepared to die for his beliefs (Ambury, 2022).
19. **B. Hoplites.** When we think of Greek warriors, we often picture the hoplite with his spear and Hoplon shield advancing in a phalanx, or tight line formation, with his fellow infantry. All Greek city-states with armies used hoplites (Olenik, 2018).
20. **B. Mt. Olympus.** The 12 Olympians are Zeus, Hera, Poseidon, Demeter, Hephaestus, Athena, Aphrodite, Ares, Apollo, Artemis, Hermes, and either Hestia or Dionysus, who joined the Olympians later (Greek Legends and Myths, 2018).
21. **D. 776 B.C.** The Pan-Greek Olympic games may have been held for as many as 500 years by this time, but the first one on record was held in the Greek city-state of Elis in the 8th Century B.C. Unlike modern Olympic games, there was no torch lighting ceremony (History.com Editors, 2019h).
22. **B. The Peloponnesian War.** The Athenian Navy was powerful enough to keep Athens as the strongest city-state. Sparta developed its navy to be more competitive, though, and eventually won the struggle for dominance in Greece (National Geographic Society, 2022e).
23. **A. Athens.** Cleisthenes introduced his revolutionary system of demokratia to Athens in 507 B.C. This "rule by the people" leveled the playing field for some, but not all. Only free male citizens over the age of 18 had voting power in ancient Athens (History.com Editors, 2018u).
24. **B. Knucklebones.** Though they were initially made with real bones from various animals, people began making knucklebones out of stone, metal, and even glass. Children played many games with them, while grown women often used them for fortune telling and grown men for gambling (Good, 2021).

Questions

25. This ancient temple to the goddess Athena is still the most famous of all the structures at Athens's Acropolis.
    a. The Pantheon
    b. Athena Major
    c. The Parthenon
    d. Olympia
26. Greek myth contains many animal mash-ups and hybrids, including this winged horse.
    a. Unicorn
    b. Narwhal
    c. Pegasus
    d. Centaur
27. The Ancient Greeks celebrated Dionysus, god of wine, fertility, madness, and the theater, with four main festivals: Lesser Dionysia, Lenea, Greater Dionysia, and…
    a. Anthesteria
    b. Fall Rush
    c. Mardi Gras
    d. Ampelos
28. Although the Ancient Greeks also had shorter, so-called Satyr plays, the two main genres in their theaters were Comedy and…
    a. Mayhem
    b. Scholarship
    c. Tragedy
    d. Philosophy
29. The marathon race is named after a Greek town—and an ancient battle that was held there. Who were the Athenians fighting at Marathon in 490 B.C.?
    a. Egyptians
    b. Syrians
    c. Spartans
    d. Persians
30. The famous Temple of Artemis at Ephesus was central to Ancient Greek religious life, although it's located in modern-day…
    a. Italy
    b. Turkey
    c. Czech Republic
    d. Armenia
31. Though the playwrights were Athenian, tragedies like *Oedipus the King, Antigone,* and *Bacchae* all draw on myths from this often-forgotten Greek city-state.
    a. Athens
    b. Crete
    c. Thebes
    d. Ibiza
32. This Spartan king is still famous for his courage, leadership, and self-sacrifice at the Battle of Thermopylae in 480 B.C.
    a. Leonidas
    b. Alexander
    c. Aristotle
    d. Demosthenes

Answers

25. **C. The Parthenon.** The famous politician Pericles ordered work to begin on the Parthenon in 447 B.C. Another, older temple existed on the site beforehand but was may have been destroyed by the ravages of war (History.com Editors, 2018b).
26. **C. Pegasus.** This immortal, winged horse is said to have sprung from the neck of Medusa, the snake-haired gorgon, when she was killed by the hero Perseus. Pegasus has been woven into the fabric of Greek myth and modern pop culture ever since (Kapach, 2023).
27. **A. Anthesteria.** This three-day festival led up to an early spring full moon. Day one was the solemn opening and tasting of new jars of wine. Day two involved drinking to excess—and a public drinking contest. Day three involved honoring the dead while also protecting the living from them (Burdrovich, 2020).
28. **C. Tragedy.** Greek tragedies like Antigone and Oedipus the King explored universal human themes like loss, grief, death, and fear for the entire community. Athens's Greater Dionysia was the most famous theater festival in its time. Theater, like today's media, was a way to explore the issues at the heart of Greek society, process them, and even complain about them (Englert, 2019).
29. **D. Persians.** At the Battle of Marathon, Athenians defeated a large force sent by Darius I in an attempt to subjugate Greece—the first of two major Persion invasions. The messenger who ran the 25 miles from the battlefield to Athens is said to have dropped dead once he delivered his good news (Nix, 2014).
30. **B. Turkey.** The Temple of Artemis at Ephesus was said to be 4 times larger than the Parthenon and was one of the Seven Wonders of the Ancient World. Ephesus passed from Greek hands into Persian, then to Alexander the Great, then to Egypt, then Roman, then finally Ottoman rule (History.com Editors, 2018i).
31. **C. Thebes.** Not to be confused with the Egyptian city of Thebes, this Greek city-state was all but destroyed when it made the mistake of siding with the invading Persians against their neighboring rivals, the Athenians. Most of what we know about Ancient Thebes is from myth, poetry, and song; there are no prominent local histories (Cartledge, 2020).
32. **A. Leonidas.** The Persian King Xerxes I, Darius's son, got up a second major invasion of Greece by both land and sea. To get inland, the Persians needed to move through a bottle-neck at Thermopylae; Leonidas's war band, though ultimately outmaneuvered, made their last stand there (History.com Editors, 2009t).

Questions

33. In Greek myth, the Minotaur, a half-man half-bull creature, was born to a queen of this island.
    a. Crete
    b. Mykonos
    c. Santorini
    d. Rhodes
34. This kingdom covered the north of Greece and much of the Balkan peninsula Under Philip II. This famous son of his expanded the empire even further.
    a. Theseus
    b. Perseus
    c. Alexander
    d. Aristotle
35. Aristotle, the great philosopher and student of Plato, codified the long-discussed belief that everything in the universe was made up of four elements. These four classical elements are…
    a. Red, Blue, Yellow, and Green
    b. Air, Water, Earth, and Fire
    c. Salt, Water, Sulfur, and Quicksilver
    d. Aether, Metal, Fire, and Lightning
36. Tradition holds that Rome was founded on April 21, 753 B.C., by these mythical twin brothers.
    a. Romulus and Remus
    b. Castor and Pollux
    c. Fred and George
    d. Tiber and Rubicon
37. Another foundation myth suggests that Rome was first settled by this mythical Trojan hero—the only Trojan that lived through Homer's epic Greek *Iliad* about the Trojan War.
    a. Achilles
    b. Hercules
    c. Augustus
    d. Aeneas
38. Written records no longer exist from the Roman Period of Kings, from the city's founding to 510 B.C., but we do know that Romulus is considered the first of those kings, and the last is…
    a. Tarquin the Proud
    b. Lucius Junius Brutus
    c. Julius Caesar
    d. Livy
39. At first, only the upper classes of Roman society, the Patricians, could hold public office and be members of this law-making body.
    a. The War Council
    b. The Senate
    c. The House of Representatives
    d. The Republicans
40. Between 264 and 164 B.C., Rome fought this series of wars with the city state of Carthage for dominance in the Mediterranean.
    a. The Trojan Wars
    b. The Wars of the Roses
    c. The Punic Wars
    d. The Hundred Years War

Answers

33. **A. Crete.** When Queen Pasiphae gave birth to the Minotaur, King Minos had the creature locked away in an ingenious labyrinth. The maze, designed by the brilliant Daedalus, kept the Minotaur locked away, but he still needed to be fed humans (Lesso, 2022).
34. **C. Alexander.** Alexander the Great came to his father Philip's throne at the age of 20. By the time he died at 32, he'd expanded his empire all the way to India (History.com Editors, 2023).
35. **B. Air, Water, Earth, and Fire.** Aether, which is included in some descriptions, originally was a part of "air," being the element that takes up the space where the others do not exist (Carr, n.d.).
36. **A. Romulus and Remus.** The sons of a princess-turned-Vestal-Virgin and the war god Mars, Romulus and Remus are said to have narrowly escaped drowning by their uncle, a king. They were kept alive by a she-wolf who suckled them until they were found by a shepherd (History.com Editors, 2019c).
37. **D. Aeneas.** Virgil, the great Roman poet, wrote his own epic about Aeneas's journey to Rome, his Aeneid, in 30–19 B.C. Interest was high just then, since Julius Caesar and his successor, the first emperor, Augustus, claimed descent from Aeneas.
38. **A. Tarquin the Proud.** From its inception, the kings of Rome were never from Rome. Tarquin was part of an Etruscan dynasty of the same name, and mostly remembered for scandal and tyranny. After Tarquin the Proud's exile, Rome instituted the Republic instead of a new dynasty (Gill, 2019).
39. **B. The Senate.** Eventually, the plebeians, or common people of Rome, gained a legislative voice in the Council of Plebs and the tribal assemblies. This style of Republican government has inspired many other political systems up to the modern age (National Geographic Society, 2022i).
40. **C. The Punic Wars.** Over the course of a century, Rome built up its navy to take on Carthage's mighty fleet. Though Roman victories were limited, and the Carthaginian General Hannibal actually invaded Italy (with elephants!) by land to devastating effect, Rome destroyed Carthage entirely in 146 B.C. (History.com Editors, 2009g).

Questions

41. These six women kept the flame of Vesta burning in her temple during their thirty-year tenure as…
    a. Vestal Virgins
    b. Pleiades
    c. House Maids
    d. Fire Maidens
42. This dictator-for-life died in 87 B.C., his legacy a warning for those who loved the Republic and an inspiration for those who would wield absolute power in Rome.
    a. Charles V
    b. Sulla
    c. Brutus
    d. Cicero
43. Many of Rome's politicians clung to the ideals of the Republic. For this reason, many of them conspired to assassinate this statesman, general, and dictator-for-life in 44 B.C.
    a. Remus
    b. Julius Caesar
    c. Nero
    d. Claudius
44. Through the Trojan hero Aneas, Julius Caesar and his great-nephew and heir, first Emperor Caesar Augustus, claimed descent from this goddess.
    a. Venus
    b. Diana
    c. Arachne
    d. Minerva
45. Roman historians tended to color their facts with the values of times. As a result, most women with political influence have been vilified, including Caesar Augustus's trusted wife Livia and this mother of the infamous Emperor Nero.
    a. Julia
    b. Calpurnia
    c. Agrippina the Younger
    d. Cleopatra
46. This center of Roman religion sat on the Capitoline hill, the most prestigious location in the whole city.
    a. The Temple of Apollo
    b. The Forge of Vulcan
    c. The Temple of Jupiter Optimus Maximus
    d. The Temple of Vesta
47. In the year 96, Rome saw the first of the Five Good Emperors come to power. These were Nerva, Trajan, Hadrian, Antoninus Pius, and this warrior-philosopher.
    a. Marcus Aurelius
    b. Mark Antony
    c. Caligula
    d. Gaius Marius
48. Roman leaders throughout the vast Empire were expected to sponsor games, both to entertain the people and to honor the gods and heroes of the past. These well-trained fighters often served as a main attraction, along with executions and exotic animals.
    a. Hoplites
    b. Gladiators
    c. Spartans
    d. Legionnaires

Answers

41. **A. Vestal Virgins.** These six priestesses of Vesta took vows of chastity on pain of death. In return, they lived a privileged life of service to their goddess, free of the heavy bonds of Roman marriage (DiGrado, 2005).
42. **B. Sulla.** A Roman general of great renown, Sulla claimed to want to restore the Republic from a period of chaos and disintegration. Most who claimed these powers in the past had them for a brief emergency period. Sulla, often called a tyrant for his brutal methods, held onto them for the rest of his life (Johns, 2023).
43. **B. Julius Caesar.** After a long and illustrious military career in Gaul and North Africa, Caesar was declared dictator-for-life in 46 B.C. He was famously assassinated, stabbed to death by dozens of Republican-minded Roman senators who claimed he was a tyrant (National Geographic Society, 2022h).
44. **A. Venus.** The Roman name for the Greek goddess Aphrodite is Venus. This goddess appears many times in Virgil's *Aeneid* to help her son Aneas, although she's unaware that his ultimate destiny is to found the city of Rome (The Getty Museum, n.d.).
45. **C. Agrippina the Younger.** Agrippina had a top-notch Roman pedigree and a line of strong women behind her. Through her brother Emperor Caligula, marriage to her uncle Emperor Claudius, and eventually her son Nero, Agrippina the Younger exercised uncommon influence on politics and world events (Bileta, 2021).
46. **C. The Temple of Jupiter Optimus Maximus.** This temple was both started and completed during the Roman Period of Kings by the Tarquins. It not only served as a place to worship the three deities of Rome—Jupiter, Juno, and Minerva—but was also the original meeting-place for the Senate (Wellesley Art Department, 2017).
47. **A. Marcus Aurelius.** The Five Good Emperors ruled during a time of expansion and prosperity for the Roman Empire. Marcus Aurelius is perhaps the most fondly remembered, as he's also a leading philosopher of the Stoic school, still revered today for his *Meditations* (Sellars, 2002).
48. **B. Gladiators.** Gladiators were a popular form of entertainment, often hero-worshiped like the movie stars of their age in spite of being on the lowest level of Roman society as slaves (UNRV, 2019).

Questions

49. Ancient Rome's most famous condiment was this sauce, made of fermented fish, salt, and herbs.
    a. Curry
    b. Gravy
    c. Ketchup
    d. Garum
50. While the Western Roman Empire came to an end in the year 476, the Eastern Roman Empire lived on under this better-known name.
    a. The Ottoman Empire
    b. The Mughal Empire
    c. The Seleucid Empire
    d. The Byzantine Empire

Answers

49. **D. Garum.** This pungent sauce was produced en masse and shipped all over the Roman empire. Modern archaeologists and culinary anthropologists have used well-preserved examples from the destroyed city of Pompeii to recreate the ancient recipe (Gresco, 2021).
50. **D. The Byzantine Empire.** The Christian Emperor Constantine I declared that his united, "new Rome" would be headquartered in Byzantium. Its longtime capital, Constantinople (modern-day Istanbul), endured until 1453 (History.com Editors, 2018ad).

Chapter 2:

Ancient Asia's Greatest Hits: China, Japan, and India

To call anything "Asian" is perhaps one of the world's largest and most inaccurate generalizations, considering the size and depth of human civilization on this vast continent. The oldest urban civilizations we know of, Indus Valley and Mesopotamia, flourished in Asia. The Persian, Mongol, and Chinese empires were a constant source of conflict, change, and innovation for millenia. Their reaches stretched far beyond their own territories as stories, cultural artifacts, and ideas traveled westward into Europe.

It'd be impossible to cover all of Asian history in a book like this—that'd be a whole series of trivia books itself! Instead, we'll explore some greatest hits. First, India, which in ancient times covers Pakistan, Bangladesh, and sometimes Nepal, as these are modern countries. Some of the world's oldest religions developed in South Asia, as well as many early human innovations like mathematics and language. Ancient China, separated from India by the mighty Himalayas, developed its own culture and language simultaneously. Constant power struggles lived side-by-side with unparalleled artistic innovation in ancient China. Japan got its start as a nation much later, which makes it an interesting case study. Although life on its islands was at first somewhat isolated, it was later influenced by the other two in powerful ways—and exerted its own influence, in the end.

While there's much more to ancient Asia than what we can cover in this one chapter, I hope this will serve as a good starting point. These ancient and powerful civilizations have given the world so much, it's nice to be able to recognize them for it in some small way.

Questions

1. This mythical Chinese emperor is said to be the father of both Chinese agricultural technology and medicine.
    a. Shen Nong
    b. Kublai Khan
    c. Qin Shi Huangdi
    d. Jie of Xia
2. The oldest evidence of silk found in China dates from the…
    a. Xia dynasty (2070–1600 B.C.)
    b. Neolithic period (c. 8500–c. 2000 B.C.)
    c. Western Zhou dynasty (1046–771 B.C.)
    d. Eastern Zhou dynasty (771–256 B.C.)
3. Early Chinese religion during the Shang Dynasty (1600–1050 B.C.) relied largely on the guidance of…
    a. Dragons
    b. The Ancestors
    c. Buddha
    d. Philosophers
4. This teacher and philosopher who lived in the 4th and 5th century B.C. had a massive impact on Chinese culture with his ideas about filial piety and moral wisdom.
    a. Hannibal
    b. Li Bai
    c. Wu Cheng'en
    d. Confucious
5. Lao-tzu, or "old master," also lived in the 5th century B.C. His teachings laid the foundation for this influential school of thought and spirituality.
    a. Daoism
    b. Stoicism
    c. Kung Fu
    d. Buddhism
6. This first Emperor of China is world famous for his elaborate tomb and its Terracotta Army, meant to guard him in the afterlife, and for conceiving the Great Wall.
    a. Confucius
    b. Qin Shi Huangdi
    c. Xi'an
    d. Zao Gao
7. The Great Wall of China kept many different foes at bay during different periods, but in the 3rd century B.C., it was reportedly built to keep out these people.
    a. Mongols
    b. Huns
    c. Rus
    d. Gauls
8. This major trade route allowed China not only to import and export goods to and from the west, but also allowed a flow of ideas and religions, like Buddhism.
    a. Route 66
    b. The Northwest Passage
    c. The Silk Road
    d. The Nile

Answers

1. **A. Shen Nong.** This "Divine Farmer" is also known as Yan Di. Though we have no contemporary accounts from the Xia dynasty (before 1500 B.C.), which is why it's considered the mythical era, tales of Shen Nong lived then. He's said to have discovered the medicinal properties of the tea plant in 2737 B.C. (Yee, n.d.).
2. **B. Neolithic Period.** The oldest example of silk still extant is from modern-day Henan Province back in 3630 B.C. In legend, silk was invented by the Yellow Emperor's wife, Lady Hsi-Ling-Shi (Silk-road.com, 2018).
3. **B. The Ancestors.** From oracle bones uncovered in the Shang capital of Anyang, modern scholars have learned that Shangdi, god and Supreme Ancestor, communicated his wishes through mystics and the king, who also served as priest (History.com Editors, 2018q).
4. **D. Confucius.** In his *Analects*, compiled by disciples after his death in 479 B.C., Confucius gives anecdotes and aphorisms meant to help people examine their own moral character (History.com Editors, 2019g).
5. **A. Daoism.** "Dao" means a way or a path, and Daoists see humanity as a small part of the larger whole of nature. Unlike Confucianism, which focused on civilization, Daoism focused on acting in accordance with nature rather than against it (Bloom, 2009).
6. **B. Qin Shi Huangdi.** He united warring bands and states into the first iteration of the country that would become China, which is why his name translates to First Emperor Qin (Lubow, 2009).
7. **B. Huns.** At that time, the Huns or Xiongnu were a nomadic people, excellent on horseback (some say they even slept on horseback!) and living in small groups led by individual chieftains (History.com Editors, 2018d).
8. **C. The Silk Road.** Buddhism traveled with Indian and Nepali monks like Bodhidarma along these well-traveled paths. When it reached China around the year 150, it came into contact with Confucianism and Daoism to form the basis for mainstream Chinese spirituality (Nanji & Niyozov, 2019).

Questions

9. This fourth-generation Confucian philosopher lived during the Warring States Period (403–221 B.C.) and believed in the inherent goodness of humanity.
    a. Xavier
    b. Mencius
    c. Sun-Tzu
    d. Xiao Long
10. Chinese craftsmen made this major technological innovation around the 2nd century B.C., and it soon spread west to revolutionize writing all over the world.
    a. Paper
    b. Clay
    c. Etching tools
    d. The Stylus
11. This sect of Buddhist monks developed and practiced martial arts as a way of sharpening mental and physical focus and ability—as well as for self-defense.
    a. Theravada
    b. Shaolin
    c. Jeet Kun Do
    d. Wu Shu
12. At this epic battle, the northern Han general Cao Cao chained his superior fleet together on the Yangtze—and the southern empires burned it all down by sailing a few flaming ships into them.
    a. The Battle of Red Cliffs
    b. The Battle of Agincourt
    c. The Battle of the River
    d. The Battle of Ya Men
13. The first part of the Eastern Zhou period, from about 771–476 B.C., is called "The Spring and Autumn period" because…
    a. The weather was very mild all year around during these centuries.
    b. The queen loved springtime.
    c. The first book of recorded Chinese history, *The Spring and Autumn Annals*, is from this time.
    d. Art and textiles from this period display spring and autumn scenes exclusively.
14. Though there's no evidence that he actually existed, this Eastern Zhou general is said to have composed *The Art of War* sometime between 475–221 B.C.
    a. Iroh
    b. Sun-Tzu
    c. Cao Cao
    d. Qin Shi Huangdi
15. This Empress of the Tang Period started out as the lowest-ranking of the emperor's consorts and rose to rule in her own right.
    a. Empress Tang
    b. Empress Tian Shu
    c. Empress Cixi
    d. Empress Wu
16. During the Tang period (618–906), monasteries could mass-produce Buddhist texts via this method.
    a. Woodblock Printing
    b. Laser Printing
    c. Movable Type Printing
    d. Etching

Answers

9. **B. Mencius.** Meng-zi or "master Meng" is often called "The Second Sage," since his importance in developing Confucian thought is second only to Confucius himself (Van Norden, 2019)
10. **A. Paper.** Before paper, the ancient Chinese kept records on bamboo strips. It was first used for packaging, but by the 4th century, paper had become the writing material of choice in China (Hansen, 2002).
11. **B. Shaolin.** These monks could defend themselves and their temples from street robbers—and sometimes their own government—as well as meditate for hours, which can be physically and mentally punishing (Kim, 2002).
12. **A. The Battle of Red Cliffs.** With the Han empire falling apart, Cao Cao tried to gather what he could and reunite China under his banner. The burning of his fleet at the Battle of Red Cliffs (in the year 208) assured that he would not (Mills, 2023).
13. **C. The first book of recorded Chinese history, *The Spring and Autumn Annals*, is from this time.** The Eastern Zhou picked up where the Western Zhou left off, moving their capital and rulers east. The Annals tell of the first part of this new rule year-by-year (Lumen Learning, 2019).
14. **B. Sun-Tzu.** Even though we're not sure Sun-Tzu (also called Sunzi) existed, whoever wrote The Art of War laid out strategy and tactics that have been used ever since, regardless of how military technology advances (National Geographic Society, 2022k).
15. **D. Empress Wu.** Wu Zetian had her first taste of real power when she married Emperor Gaozong. After his death and the death of their son, she continued to rule efficiently and decisively on her own from 690–705 (Dash, 2012).
16. **A. Woodblock printing.** As early as the year 650, Tang printers began developing woodblocks as a method of mass-producing scrolls and books. Calendars and almanacs were sanctioned by the state, unlike the Buddhist texts the monasteries were producing (History.com Editors, 2018r).

Questions

17. This stone was highly prized in ancient China by royalty and nobles, even more than gold and silver. It was believed to have protective powers in death, too.
    a. Alabaster
    b. Onyx
    c. Granite
    d. Jade
18. Chan Buddhism, which focuses more on immediate meditation than deep reflection on texts, was developed in China around the 6th century—but it's better known by this Japanese name.
    a. Zen
    b. Shaolin
    c. Judo
    d. Shintō
19. This indigenous Tibetan religion existed on the plateau for centuries before Indian monks introduced Buddhism in the 6th century.
    a. Hinduism
    b. Jainism
    c. Bön
    d. Humanism
20. Harappa and Mohenjo-Daro are ancient cities excavated in modern-day Pakistan, and representatives of this Bronze Age human civilization in South Asia.
    a. Mesopotamia
    b. Indus Valley
    c. Egyptian
    d. Persian
21. This oldest of the sacred Hindu Vedas or religious texts was compiled into one book between 1500–1200 B.C., but the hymns it collects are probably much older than that.
    a. Rig Veda
    b. Bhagavad Gita
    c. Mandala
    d. Atharva Veda
22. Hindus believe this ancient language, the source of many modern Indian languages and the language of the Vedas, is eternal, with no beginning or end.
    a. Greek
    b. Sanskrit
    c. Hindi
    d. Tamil
23. The 16 Mahajanapadas or "great realms" of ancient India in the 6th century B.C., are referenced in important religious texts of the time, like ancient India's longest epic poem…
    a. The Odyssey
    b. Mahabharata
    c. Vikram and the Vampire
    d. Amar Chitra Katha
24. This empire under Darius the Great annexed the Indus Valley in 518 B.C.
    a. Persian
    b. Mongol
    c. Roman
    d. Merovingian

Answers

17. **D. Jade.** Even early, Neolithic peoples of China like the Hongshan, prized this smooth, green stone, using it for ornaments similar to those worn by modern jade fans (The British Museum, 2016).
18. **A. Zen.** Chan Buddhist texts make use of a particular literary device called a gong-an (Japanese koan) or "public case" discussion between master and student to introduce ideas (Hershock, 2015).
19. **C. Bön.** Though there's some question about whether Bön practitioners considered it a religion in the strictest sense before Buddhism appeared, it refers to the animistic and shamanistic indigenous spirituality of Tibet (Powers, 1995).
20. **B. Indus Valley.** This ancient civilization thrived between 2500–1900 B.C. in what's now Pakistan. The urban centers built by the Indus Valley or Harappan civilization have many standardized conveniences across the board, including standard brick sizes, streets, and even sewer systems. (PBS, 2009).
21. **A. Rig Veda.** There are four major Vedas in Hinduism. The Rig Veda, the oldest and one of the first if not the first human book of knowledge, is a collection of hymns of praise to gods (Tiwari, 2023).
22. **B. Sanskrit.** Hindu tradition says Sanskrit was made by God. Linguists believe its parent-language came from somewhere to the northwest of India, possibly Syria, and eventually evolved into Vedic Sanskrit (Daniyal, 2015).
23. **B. Mahabharata.** This epic poem tells of a war between two branches of the ruling family of the Mahajanapada of Kuru, the Pandavas and the Kauravas. It's the longer of the two great ancient Hindu epics (Ranjan, 2023).
24. **A. Persian.** Darius I or Darius the Great was the third King of Kings of the Persian Achaemenid dynasty. Centuries later, parts of India were conquered again by Persian-speaking kings, the Mughals (PBS, 2009).

Questions

25. This religion preaches non-violence and honors 24 Jinas, including Mahavira, the final Jina, who was born around 599 B.C.
    a. Bahai
    b. Islam
    c. Jainism
    d. Hinduism
26. This man's army brought a heavy Greek influence into northern India in the 320s B.C.
    a. Akbar the Great
    b. Odysseus
    c. Menelaus
    d. Alexander the Great
27. This first great pan-Indian empire was ruled first by Chandragupta and later by Ashoka.
    a. Kushana
    b. Malla
    c. Pallava
    d. Maurya
28. From the 4th century B.C., countless Tamil poems and songs were composed at Sangams, or poet-gatherings, in this ancient temple city.
    a. Madurai
    b. Athens
    c. Varanasi
    d. Puducherry
29. This modern-day Indian state takes its name from the Chera dynasty, who ruled along the southwestern coast during the Sangam period (600 B.C.–300 C.E.) and beyond.
    a. Andhra Pradesh
    b. Kerala
    c. Kushana
    d. Tamilakam
30. This classical dance form was developed around 400 B.C. in modern day Tamil Nadu—and it's still going strong today.
    a. Ballet
    b. Dakini
    c. Bharatanatyam
    d. Tanjore
31. Soon after Buddhism split into two sects, the famous Kushana King Kanishka adopted this sect, which became the most popular and was exported all over Asia.
    a. Mahayana
    b. Zen
    c. Vaishnavism
    d. Jainism
32. This massive earth-and-stone dam was commissioned by King Karikala Chola in the 2nd century and is still in use today.
    a. Hoover Dam
    b. Victoria Dam
    c. Grand Anicut Dam
    d. Colombo Dam

Answers

25. **C. Jainism.** Mahavira or "the great hero" was born Vardhamana, of the warrior class rather than the priestly class. According to Jainism, he fasted and meditated for 12 years to achieve enlightenment (National Geographic Society, 2022b).
26. **D. Alexander the Great.** Not long before his death, Alexander led his conquering army into India and prevailed at the Battle of the Hydaspes or Battle of Jhelum (326 B.C.). His army refused to go any further from home, after that. Alexander's empire was divided among his four most trusted generals, known as the Diadochi (Wickramasinghe, 2021).
27. **D. Maurya.** Chandragupta Maurya stepped into the power vacuum left after Alexander died. His grandson, Ashoka, started his own rule as a bloodthirsty expansionist, only to have a change of heart and mind after converting to Buddhism (National Geographic Society, 2022d).
28. **A. Madurai.** The Pandya dynasty of Tamil kings sponsored Sangams in Madurai long before they built the great Meenakshi temple there. When visiting the temple in modern times, you can still see the large reflecting pool where poets would float while throwing down in these ancient-times rap battles (National Geographic Society, 2022f).
29. **B. Kerala.** The Chera dynasty was known for trade throughout the ancient world. They ruled most of modern-day Kerala and parts of Tamil Nadu from the 1st century B.C., according to the literature of the time (National Geographic Society, 2022f).
30. **C. Bharatnatyam.** This codified dance form consists of basic steps called adavus and hand gestures or mudras. It's practiced all over the world now, thanks to the Indian diaspora (Lo Iacono, 2020).
31. **A. Mahayana.** Mahayana ("greater vehicle") Buddhism developed a separate identity from Hinayana ("lesser vehicle") or Theravada Buddhism between the years 100 and 500 (PBS, 2008a).
32. **C. Grand Anicut Dam.** This dam, also called Kallanai, creates a fertile and rich delta from the Cauvery River in Tamil Nadu to this very day (PBS, 2008a).

Questions

33. Rock-cut temples at these two sites were carved into the stone during the Gupta Empire's wide rule over north India (320–647).
    a. Mumbai and Delhi
    b. Babylon and Bangalore
    c. Varanasi and Lumbini
    d. Ajanta and Elephanta
34. This large language family is believed to have originated over 4500 years ago, and to have been in South Asia long before Sanskrit and its predecessors arrived.
    a. Urdu
    b. Dravidian
    c. Indo-European
    d. Sino-Tibetan
35. This Gupta-era (320–627) center of learning and knowledge in Bihar was lost for centuries, until archaeologists rediscovered its ruins in 1860.
    a. University of Madras
    b. Cambridge University
    c. Naropa University
    d. Nalanda University
36. The Indian game chaturanga, invented sometime before the 6th century, is the precursor for this beloved modern game.
    a. Boggle
    b. Chess
    c. Parcheesi
    d. Scrabble
37. This neolithic period of Japanese history is named for the earthenware or unfired pottery its scattered people produced.
    a. Jōmon Period
    b. Joseon Period
    c. Osaka Period
    d. Pottery Period
38. The cultivation of this domesticated crop is thought to be a factor in Japan's Yayoi culture (c. 300 B.C.–300) becoming more settled and agricultural.
    a. Corn
    b. Wheat
    c. Plums
    d. Rice
39. This legendary Japanese kingdom is said to have existed during the Yayoi period (c. 300 B.C.–300), ruled over by the magical Queen Himiko.
    a. Atlantis
    b. Yamatai
    c. Kyushu
    d. Momotarō
40. This long-ruling dynasty lends its name to the period of Japanese history from 250–710.
    a. Osaka
    b. Kyoto
    c. Yamato
    d. Baekje

Answers

33. **D. Ajanta and Elephanta.** While the cave-temple complex at Ajanta is Buddhist, the one at Elephanta contains both Buddhist and Hindu iconography, showing the similarities and differences between them (Manon, n.d.).
34. **B. Dravidian.** This language family includes modern Kannada, Malayalam, Telugu, and Tamil. Tamil, the oldest of these, is considered one of the classical languages of the world (Kolipakam et al., 2018).
35. **D. Nalanda University.** Although founded as a Buddhist learning center, Nalanda also taught the arts, medicine, math and astronomy, politics and warfare. It was founded in 427 (AICTE, n.d.).
36. **B. Chess.** Chaturanga was a war strategy board game based on the four military divisions: infantry, cavalry, elephantry, and chariotry. Now, those have turned into pawns, knights, rooks, and bishops. In modern times, Indians take pride in the game and often work hard to become masters of international chess (Kale, 2021).
37. **A. Jōmon Period.** Scattered hunter-gatherer groups occupied the island as early as 30000 B.C., which is Paleolithic. Early agricultural evidence begins cropping up around 5000 B.C., which is comfortably Neolithic (Department of Asian Art, 2019a).
38. **D. Rice.** Wet-rice paddy cultivation techniques arrived from China through Korea sometime before the 1st century B.C., and were probably integral in people making the decision to settle down in permanent villages surrounding their crops (Department of Asian Art, 2019b).
39. **B. Yamatai.** This mythical kingdom is as argued about as Atlantis in the western world. Queen Himiko uses sorcery to control the people in the stories but she also brings peace and great prosperity (Runnebaum, 2015).
40. **C. Yamato.** This centuries-long era saw rapid introduction of new ideas melding with old ones, and is divided into two eras: the Kofun (250–538) and Asuka (538–710) (University of Pittsburgh, n.d.).

Questions

41. Before Buddhism appeared on Japan's shores, this indigenous religion flourished.
    a. Shintō
    b. Bön
    c. Mithraism
    d. Gnosticism
42. The Kofun era of Japanese history is named for these distinctive architectural features.
    a. Temples
    b. Burial Mounds
    c. Pagodas
    d. Palaces
43. Writing from this country began to enter Japan during the Kofun era (250–538) with several waves of immigrants from…
    a. China
    b. Mongolia
    c. Russia
    d. Thailand
44. These small clay figurines, used as grave goods, give us most of our information about Kofun military technology and dress.
    a. Action figures
    b. Voodoo Dolls
    c. Votives
    d. Haniwa
45. Mahayana Buddhism came to Japan via trade routes through this nearby country.
    a. Mongolia
    b. Taiwan
    c. Korea
    d. Fiji
46. When Buddhism came to Japan in the 6th century, it had this effect on the local Shintō religion.
    a. Buddhism had no effect on Shintō.
    b. Buddhism totally eclipsed Shintō.
    c. Buddhism split the country in half with Shintō.
    d. Buddhism incorporated Shintō in some ways.
47. The Buddhist Hōryūji Temple was commissioned by Emperor Jōmei in the 6th century in this city, where he's buried.
    a. Nara
    b. Kyoto
    c. Osaka
    d. Hong Kong
48. This Empress was a supporter of the relatively-new religion, Buddhism, and Japan's first historical empress regnant.
    a. Empress Wu
    b. Tomoe Gozen
    c. Empress Suiko
    d. Higuchi Ichiyō

Answers

41. **A. Shintō.** Practitioners of Shintō recognize divine spirits or kami in all things of the natural world, from trees to seasons to mountains. This practice predates historical records in Japan. (Hammer, 2019)
42. **B. Burial mounds.** A Kofun is a key-hole shaped burial mound that could either be built into a natural hill or on flat earth. Grave goods accompanied the upper-class Yamato nobles buried within them (Forest, 2018).
43. **A. China.** Japanese people who learned to write, plus Chinese and Korean immigrants (called torajin), wrote with Chinese characters during this early era (Forest, 2018).
44. **D. Haniwa.** These pottery figures were placed alongside jewels, weapons, and other grave goods with leaders buried in Kofun. Haniwa means "warrior" (Forest, 2018).
45. **C. Korea.** Then called the kingdom of Baekje, Korea was a major influence and corridor for influence into Japan at the time (Coman, n.d.).
46. **D. Buddhism incorporated Shintō in some ways.** Rather than butting heads, Shintō practitioners could follow Buddhism side-by-side. Japanese Buddhism took on a singularly Shintō iconography and vice versa (Hammer, 2019).
47. **A. Nara.** The Hōryūji complex has been a place of continuous Buddhist worship since the Asuka era. Today, Nara is a UNESCO World Heritage Site thanks to its many ancient monuments (UNESCO World Heritage Centre, n.d.).
48. **C. Empress Suiko.** She reigned from the year 592–628, when she promoted and patronized Buddhism, art, and administrative reforms. Like many female rulers in patriarchal societies, her legacy has been occasionally tarnished, but still holds up in modern eyes (Lewis, 2019).

Questions

49. Prince Shōtoku (ruled 574–622) started the process of centralizing Japan's government with this document, heavily influenced by Confucianism and Buddhism.
    a. The Seventeen-Article Constitution
    b. The Declaration of Independence
    c. Magna Carta
    d. Nihon Shoki
50. These reforms, implemented during the Asuka era (538–710) of the Yamato period, strengthened and centralized power in Japan.
    a. The Geneva Conventions
    b. Taika Reforms
    c. Nara Reforms
    d. Confucian Reforms

Answers

49. **A. The Seventeen-Article Constitution.** Unlike modern constitutions, this one doesn't so much lay out the administration of a government and laws as it provides guidelines for the behavior of people, especially toward their state and emperor (Asia for Educators, n.d.).
50. **B. Taika Reforms.** These Reforms, the Taika no Kaishin, were based on the Chinese imperial form of government. It centralized political and social administration radically (Coman, n.d.).

Chapter 3:

The Not-So-Dark Ages: Knights and the Middle Ages

The phrase "Dark Ages" often calls to mind a Monty Python sketch of a corpse wagon being dragged through muddy streets crawling with filthy peasants and animals. While that's obviously satire, it's not far off what most people really think. This innovative, culturally rich period, between the 5th and 15th century in Europe, has suffered from being relegated to "the middle," a time between Classical brilliance and Renaissance rediscovery of Classical brilliance.

It's so much more than that, though. After the fall of the Western Roman Empire, which had knitted most of Europe together at one point or another, massive power vacuums opened up. In some places, indigenous people, classified as "barbarians" by Rome, got their power back, giving rise to powerful new nations. In others, invasions from nearby and far off parts succeeded in filling the political void. Trade with the east brought new luxuries, ideas, and interests to the courts and people of Europe. The Catholic Church rose to new heights of power, positioning itself as the supreme power in Europe and inciting the Crusades. Deadly plagues swept through, fundamentally changing not just the way people thought about life and death, but also showing the cracks in the economic feudal system.

It was a time of great contradictions: of political empowerment and enslavement, of the celebration of art and the stratification of society. A fascinating time, and the real genesis of the modern Europe we know to this day. Yes, it's true, the idea of "going medieval" on something or someone is pretty dark. But the medieval period itself, the middle ages, had its glaringly bright spots, and they deserve to be remembered, too.

Questions

1. The medieval period or middle ages is commonly reckoned to have begun with this major event in the year 476.
    a. The birth of Genghis Khan
    b. The fall of the Western Roman Empire
    c. The battle of Agincourt
    d. The siege of Acre
2. It's uncertain why these people came to Britain after the Roman empire left, but they soon took administrative center stage among the Celtic Britons and Romano-British.
    a. The Anglo-Saxons
    b. The Huns
    c. The Vikings
    d. The Gauls
3. This Frankish king defeated the last Roman ruler of Gaul, Syagrius, in 486. He went on to unite even more Frankish tribes and found the seminal Merovingian dynasty.
    a. Louis XIV
    b. Henri I
    c. Charles V
    d. Clovis I
4. Justinian the Great reigned over this empire from 527–65, strengthening it and solidifying its commitment to Christian Eastern Orthodoxy.
    a. Byzantine
    b. Mughal
    c. Mongol
    d. Ottoman
5. The Prophet Muhammad was born in this city in the year 570.
    a. Baghdad
    b. Mecca
    c. Jerusalem
    d. Abu Dhabi
6. Muslim Arab and Berber raiders established a presence in modern-day Spain as early as 714, and they called it this, meaning "Land of the Vandals."
    a. Toledo
    b. Barcelona
    c. Moors
    d. Al-Andalus
7. Monastic life varied wildly in the early middle ages, but this particular set of rules for religious communities spread well beyond its point of origin at the Abbey of Montecassino, near Rome, in the 6th century.
    a. The Golden Rule
    b. Benedictine Rule
    c. King David's Rule
    d. Patience and Prudence
8. Pepin the Short deposed the last Merovingian king of the Frankish empire, starting the Carolingian dynasty, best known for his son…
    a. Karol
    b. Charles V
    c. Wenceslaus
    d. Charlemagne

Answers

1. **B. The fall of the Western Roman Empire.** The empire centered on the city of Rome itself—as opposed to the Eastern Roman Empire centered in Constantinople (now Istanbul), which carried on throughout the middle ages (History.com Editors, 2010c).
2. **A. The Anglo-Saxons.** Angles, Saxons, Jutes, and people from other warlike groups from modern-day Germany and southern Scandinavia migrated to modern-day England in the late 5th century. There are conflicting theories as to how and why they made this migration. Some think that they were hired by leftover Romano-British leaders to fight off invasions from Ireland and Scotland—and when they weren't paid properly, they just stayed. Others suggest their continental lands flooded or were otherwise made unlivable—and we do have evidence of abandoned Anglo-Saxon villages from that time period (Mason, 2018).
3. **D. Clovis I.** Clovis is remembered not only for gathering all the Franks under his rule for the first time, a precursor to the modern country of France, but also for his conversion to Catholicism (Snell, 2020).
4. **A. Byzantine.** Also known as the Eastern Roman Empire, it thrived while its western counterpart disintegrated in Rome. In English, the word "Byzantine" is today often used to describe something elaborate or complicated. This is a reference to the elaborate, beautiful style of Byzantine art as much as the labyrinth of political machinations at the Byzantine Court throughout the centuries (Brooks, 2019).
5. **B. Mecca.** Islamic texts say that the Angel Gabriel gave Muhammad his first divine revelation in the year 610, and he began preaching shortly thereafter. He gathered a modest following there, but the rich and powerful merchants who ran the city were disturbed by this new religious revolution happening in their city. He was run out of town and settled with his followers in the war-ravaged oasis now known as Medina (Brooks, 2019).
6. **D. Al-Andalus.** After the Western Roman Empire fell, the Iberian peninsula was ruled by a series of warring Vandal and Visigothic tribes, until it fell largely under exiled Umayyad leadership from Syria (Dodds, 1992).
7. **B. Benedictine Rule.** Benedict of Nursia codified rules for his monastery at Montecassino that are often distilled into the Latin motto "Ora et labora" or *pray and work*. They're still used by many monasteries to this day (Sorabella, 2019).
8. **D. Charlemagne.** Charles the Great, as he's called in English, inherited half of Pepin the Short's Frankish kingdom—the other half went to his other son, Carloman, who died after two years of fighting his brother for control (Marshall, 1912).

Questions

9. The earliest (8th century) of these seafaring raiders from Scandinavia were looking for riches—in later years, they began to settle throughout the known world and beyond.
    a. Huns
    b. Vandals
    c. Vikings
    d. Mercians
10. This Christian Anglo-Saxon king succeeded in uniting several of the English kingdoms against the Viking invaders from his capital in Wessex, Winchester.
    a. Alfred the Great
    b. Ragnar Lothbrok
    c. Aethelstan I
    d. Harald
11. In the 911 Treaty of Saint-Clair-sur-Epte, Charles III or Charles the Simple of France granted this large swathe of land to the Viking leader Rollo and his people—in return for protection from other Vikings.
    a. Aquitaine
    b. Paris
    c. Normandy
    d. Burgundy
12. This elaborately illuminated gospel, on display today at Dublin's Trinity College, was painted with pigments made of woad, indigo, yellow orpiment, lead red, and copper green on vellum or prepared calf skin around the year 800.
    a. The King James Bible
    b. The Book of Kells
    c. The Devil's Dictionary
    d. The Coverdale Bible
13. Ancient Romans used "hipposandals," but this important military, agricultural, and transportation technology didn't take its modern form in Western Europe until about the year 1000.
    a. Horseshoes
    b. Tanks
    c. Gunpowder
    d. Nails
14. In 1066, Duke Rollo's great-great-great grandson, Duke William of Normandy, crossed the English Channel and defeated the last Anglo-Saxon king, Harold Godwinson, in this battle.
    a. The Battle of the Bulge
    b. The Battle of Antietam
    c. The Battle of Waterloo
    d. The Battle of Hastings
15. The Normans developed these eminently defensible structures, at first of the motte-and-bailey style, to defend their territories.
    a. Castles
    b. Tanks
    c. Walls
    d. Portcullises

Answers

9. **C. Vikings.** Also known as Norsemen or Northmen, these weren't a single ethnic group from a single land, but raiders from similar cultures throughout modern-day Denmark, Norway, Sweden—and possibly even Finland and Estonia (History.com Editors, 2009i).
10. **A. Alfred the Great.** Alfred fortified and organized Anglo-Saxon territory to withstand continued Viking encroachments. In 886, even Anglo-Saxons in Danelaw recognized him as King of the Anglo-Saxons, not just Wessex (Beyer, 2023).
11. **C. Normandy.** Rollo the Viking, the first Duke of Normandy, is buried in the Cathedral at Rouen. We still don't know exactly where he was born or came from. For all that, we do know he founded a line of Norman leaders that would eventually rule northern France and England (Haskew, 2015).
12. **B. The Book of Kells.** Although we can't be sure where this gorgeous manuscript was illuminated or painted, it was probably either a monastery on the island of Iona or a monastery at Kells, County Meath. Scholars think it's the work of three different monk-artists (Trinity College Dublin, 2021).
13. **A. Horseshoes.** Though protective hoof coverings of wood, leather, and fiber were common throughout the world since horses were domesticated, farriers in Europe didn't start nailing metal shoes to hooves until the middle ages. This marked a huge improvement in transportation of both goods and people (Cohen, 2002).
14. **D. The Battle of Hastings.** Duke William claimed to have been promised the throne by the previous Anglo-Saxon King of England, Edward the Confessor, who was a distant cousin of his. When Harold II took it instead, he crossed the channel and fought for England—and won (Bayeux Museum, n.d.).
15. **A. Castles.** Developed as defensive structures, the original castles were designed to be defensible by very few people for a very long siege. They also made a very loud statement for the ruling class, as the Norman castles did in England (Beyer, 2022).

Questions

16. The world, and Europe in particular, experienced population growth during a warm period between the 8th and 13th centuries, often referred to as the…
    a. Medieval Climate Optimum
    b. Global Warming
    c. Hot Centuries
    d. Opposite Ice Age
17. This system of government, common in medieval Europe as well as China and Japan during later periods, was one where all land was in the gift of the king, held by his nobility, who leased it to their vassals, who arranged for peasants or serfs to work it in exchange for protection.
    a. Communism
    b. Feudalism
    c. Socialism
    d. Oligarchy
18. These mounted, heavy cavalry warriors first appeared as servants to Frankish lords; the violence of their profession was eventually tempered by the famous code of chivalry in the 11th and 12th century.
    a. Tatars
    b. Charioteers
    c. Magyars
    d. Knights
19. The Middle Ages are often called the Dark Ages, as it was once thought much wisdom of the Classical world had been lost. In fact, many Muslim centers of learning were translating Greek classics into Arabic during this period, in particular Baghdad's…
    a. Library of Alexandria
    b. House of Wisdom
    c. University of Classics
    d. Monastery of the Sun
20. This Italian port city was founded in the 5th century, but became integral enough to world trade to split off from the Byzantine empire and become a powerhouse in its own right by the 9th century. Its connections to the east, especially via the silk road, paved the streets around St. Mark's with metaphorical gold.
    a. Florence
    b. Ravenna
    c. Naples
    d. Venice
21. Though it wasn't much of an improvement on the accuracy of the water clock, the first mechanical clock was probably invented in this century.
    a. 5th
    b. 7th
    c. 13th
    d. 18th
22. Textile making was a major occupation for women and families in the middle ages, greatly helped by this invention from the east.
    a. The spinning wheel
    b. The cotton gin
    c. The oil presser
    d. The printing press

Answers

16. **A. Medieval Climate Optimum.** Studies of tree-rings have confirmed a longstanding theory that Europe warmed up due to solar and volcanic activity during these centuries, allowing people to grow more food and populations to flourish (Björklund et al., 2023).
17. **B. Feudalism.** Although the word wasn't used in medieval times, Feudalism developed around the 8th century when Frankish kings would give lords lands (or a *fief*) for life in return for service. Knights or tenant vassals who served the lord would administer a portion of the land, which was worked by serfs or freemen, depending on the time and place. The produce of the land then made its way up the chain via taxes, which could be paid in food, money, or labor (Cartwright, 2018).
18. **D. Knights.** As this elite military class developed its own privileges, society developed rules and regulations for how a figure of such violence and power should behave toward those he served, those he loved, and those he should protect. Hence, the chivalric code (The Getty Museum, n.d.-b).
19. **B. House of Wisdom.** The Golden age of Islam centered around the Abbasid Caliphs establishment of Baghdad as a center of learning and innovation in the year 762. In 1258, Mongol invaders destroyed the great libraries of Baghdad, throwing the books into the Tiber river (Lyons, 2011).
20. **D. Venice.** This city of canals was the point of entry for many luxuries imported from the far east, maker of trade deals with otherwise hostile empires, and host to a truly sensational Carnival (UNESCO, 2019).
21. **C. 13th.** Mechanical clocks require a device called an escapement, which keeps a steady rhythm allowing it to measure the passage of time. The first escapement we know of was described in 1250 by French architect Villard de Honnecourt (Lienhard, n.d.).
22. **A. The spinning wheel.** Though this marvelous invention's point of origin is a matter of some debate, it's clear it came to Europe in the middle ages and featured heavily in economics and folk tales thereafter (Bellis, 2011).

Questions

23. In 1054, Christianity experienced a great upheaval when it split forever into two factions…
    a. Gnosticism and Evangelism
    b. Roman Catholicism and Eastern Orthodoxy
    c. Episcopalians and Anglicans
    d. Christians and Zoroastrians
24. This remarkable heiress was married to the French king Louis VII in 1137, but had her marriage annulled in 1152 and married the heir to the English throne, soon to be Henry II.
    a. Anne of Burgundy
    b. Eleanor of Aquitaine
    c. Isabella of Castile
    d. Margaret of Anjou
25. This first Habsburg Holy Roman Emperor was elected during a period of great turmoil by 7 prince-electors—under heavy orders from Pope Gregory X—in 1273.
    a. Franz Josef
    b. John I
    c. Rudolf I
    d. Charlemagne
26. His overtaxed and unhappy barons forced King John of England to sign this "great charter" in 1215.
    a. Magna Carta
    b. The Declaration of Independence
    c. The Rights of Man
    d. The Constitution
27. When Genghis Khan was born in the mid-12th century in Mongolia, he was called…
    a. Tenzin
    b. Temujin
    c. Theodore
    d. Tian Ming
28. This grandson of Genghis Khan not only became Great Khan of the Mongols, but also displaced the Chinese Song dynasty with his own, renaming it Yuan.
    a. Sun Tzu
    b. Aamir Khan
    c. Kublai Khan
    d. Batu Khan
29. Pope Urban II declared the First Crusade to unite Europe under him in an attempt to take back this city from the Seljuk Turks.
    a. Nazareth
    b. Baghdad
    c. Mecca
    d. Jerusalem
30. The Crusades brought about a new combination of monastic and military orders, giving rise to such combination orders as the Knights Templar and…
    a. The White Knights
    b. The Black Knights
    c. The Knights Hospitaller
    d. The Sovereign Order

Answers

23. **B. Roman Catholicism and Eastern Orthodoxy.** The Great Schism or the Schism of 1054 represented a final break between the Roman and Byzantine churches on matters both political and liturgical. The ultimate Christian authority in Western Europe was Rome, and in the east it was Constantinople (National Geographic Society, 2022c).
24. **B. Eleanor of Aquitaine.** While still married to Louis, Eleanor went on crusade to Antioch and was impressed by the marvels of Byzantium. She and Henry had four sons that survived to adulthood, two of whom became king (The Ohio State University, 2019).
25. **C. Rudolf I.** Rudolf was a Count from an old family of Swiss origin when he was elected Holy Roman Emperor. His later victories would bring Austria under Habsburg rule, as well. The family ruled for centuries, and though their empire was dissolved in the 20th century, there are still Habsburgs who own some of the great castles of Europe to this day (Gruber, n.d.).
26. **A. Magna Carta.** Though the charter didn't make much of a dent in what the barons saw as the excesses of King John's rule at first, it was reissued to better effect later, and eventually served as the basis for English Common Law and modern states all over the world (History.com Editors, 2009u).
27. **B. Temujin.** His mother and siblings were abandoned by their nomadic clan after the murder of their father. He survived to unite the clans of the Mongolian steppes into a powerhouse, making allies and promoting people based on loyalty and ability rather than blood ties (History.com Editors, 2009l).
28. **C. Kublai Khan.** He didn't automatically inherit the title of Great Khan after his brother Möngke died. Kublai had to leave his military campaigns in China and challenge their other brother, Ariq Boke, to win the title. Kublai was ruthless and aggressive, but he also fostered a court and empire where tolerance and learning were prized above most things.
29. **D. Jerusalem.** At the Council of Clermont in 1095, Urban II used the Muslim occupation of the Christian Holy City as a way to unite European Christians under his spiritual and ultimately political influence. While the first crusade saw some success, ultimately they petered out as subsequent Crusades continued to head east to "reclaim" what was never really theirs in the first place (History.com Editors, 2019e).
30. **C. The Knights Hospitaller.** Knights of both orders took monastic vows and were expected to protect and defend pilgrims to the Holy Land and minister to the sick and poor. While there are no more Knights Templar, there are still Hospitallers today, known as the Knights of Malta (Snell, 2021).

Questions

31. This medieval Italian philosopher and saint spent his career writing and preaching about reconciling the principles of faith and reason.
    a. Thomas Aquinus
    b. Socrates
    c. Thomas Malory
    d. Mencius
32. Chivalric literature of the middle ages focused on romances, tales of knights and magical, fairy-tale-like adventures, like those about…
    a. Hedgehogs
    b. King Arthur
    c. Saint Jerome
    d. Princess Buttercup
33. This revolutionary technology was created in China in the 9th century and brought to Europe by traders and Crusaders.
    a. Gunpowder
    b. Hand sanitizer
    c. The piano
    d. The steam engine
34. This Florentine painter of the middle ages prefigured the Renaissance by pioneering a more natural, elegant style than the gold background and stylized forms of artists before him.
    a. Michelangelo
    b. Giotto
    c. Caravaggio
    d. Picasso
35. In the 14th century, this disease ripped from east to west via trade routes, causing overnight deaths and taking out over ⅓ of Europe's population.
    a. Bubonic Plague
    b. Coronavirus
    c. Ebola virus
    d. Typhoid fever
36. The Black Death of the 14th century broke down social and class barriers all over Europe, causing uprisings like this one in Florence as workers demanded a voice in their own government.
    a. The French Revolution
    b. Medici's Rebellion
    c. The Bonfire of the Vanities
    d. The Ciompi Revolt
37. Somewhat analogous to the European knight, these Japanese warriors appeared during the Heian Period (794–1185) as service-men to wealthy landowners.
    a. Samurai
    b. Takeshi
    c. Deku
    d. Hatori
38. During the Middle Ages, communities of Jewish people began to flourish in Islamic kingdoms like Spain and Christian ones in the Rhineland. These were the ancestors of today's…
    a. Rabbinical scholars
    b. Ashkenazi Jews
    c. Bavarians
    d. Craftspeople

Answers

31. **A. Thomas Aquinus.** He said that both faith and reason came from God, and therefore weren't only compatible, but worked in concert. This was revolutionary in the history of Christian theology and philosophy, later impacting the Reformation (Biography.com Editors, 2019).
32. **B. King Arthur.** Arthur, Merlin, and the Knights of the Round Table appear in many medieval romances, including the extensive Vulgate Cycle and the romances of Chrétien de Troyes from the 12th century (Burgess, 2023).
33. **A. Gunpowder.** Saltpeter, one of the main ingredients in gunpowder, had been used for medicines in China for centuries. Once monks looking for an elixir of life mixed it with sulfur and charcoal, gunpowder was accidentally born (Brown University, 2009).
34. **B. Giotto.** Giotto di Bondone (1265–1337) painted magnificent frescoes all over the churches and chapels of Italy, first as a disciple of Cimabue and then on his own (National Gallery of Art, 2016).
35. **A. Bubonic Plague.** The Black Death, as it was called, seemed incomprehensible to minds unfamiliar with modern germ theory. People thought anything so disastrous must be a punishment from God (History.com Editors, 2010g).
36. **D. The Ciompi Revolt.** After the plague ripped through Italy, wool-workers found their labor at a premium. These *popolo minute* or little people could demand decent wages, but the ruling aristocrats didn't want to give them a political voice, too (Armstrong, 2021).
37. **A. Samurai.** Later, under the military dictatorship of the Kamakura Shogunate (1185–1333), the samurai became a real driving force and source of power in Japan (History.com Editors, 2018p).
38. **B. Ashkenazi Jews.** The largest populations of Jewish people in the Middle Ages were in the Middle East, but researchers have shown that Ashkenazi Jewish culture and people existed in Europe as early as the 300s (Curry, n.d.).

Questions

39. By the mid-13th century, a king of England like Henry III required the cooperation of this board of advisors, the precursor to today's lawmaking body, to levy new taxes.
    a. Congress
    b. The Fyrd
    c. Parliament
    d. The Estates General
40. At this battle in modern-day France, Henry V of England won back rights to parts of France long-sought-after by English Kings during the Hundred Years War.
    a. The Battle of Crecy
    b. The Battle of Agincourt
    c. The Battle of Gibraltar
    d. The Battle of Waterloo
41. This 5th Sultan of the Ottoman empire is also called its 2nd founder because he reunited the empire via conquest after it was broken up between him and his brothers.
    a. Akbar
    b. Ashoka
    c. Mehmed I
    d. Mustafa
42. This "empire" that rose from the ashes of the Frankish Carolingian Empire wasn't so much one country as dozens, eventually hundreds of smaller duchies, counties, and territories.
    a. The Holy Roman Empire
    b. The Byzantine Empire
    c. Prussia
    d. Britain
43. Years after William Wallace's Scottish rebellion was crushed in 1298, this man, Wallace's one-time ally, became King of the Scots in 1306.
    a. James VI
    b. Hugo
    c. Gustav III
    d. Robert the Bruce
44. In the late 14th Century, this massive defeat of a Franco-Hungarian army by Sultan Bayezid I all but extinguished Christian Europe's attempts to halt the expansion of the Ottoman Empire.
    a. The Battle of Acre
    b. The Battle of Nicopolis
    c. The Battle of Actium
    d. The Battle of Marathon
45. When Clement V was elected pope in 1305, largely thanks to the influence of King Philip IV of France, he was so unpopular in Rome that he moved the Papacy to this city.
    a. Avignon
    b. Lyon
    c. Babylon
    d. Constantinople
46. This series of bloody English civil wars played out between supporters of the houses of York and Lancaster from 1455–1485.
    a. The Hundred Years War
    b. The Wars of the Roses
    c. Caesar's Civil War
    d. The Peninsular War

Answers

39. **C. Parliament.** Though the first English parliament technically met when they forced King John to sign Magna Carta, they then called themselves his Great Council. This first Parliament had been chosen by the king, like a modern Prime Minister's Cabinet more than the representatives from different areas that were on it by the 1250s (History.com Editors, 2017a).
40. **B. The Battle of Agincourt.** October 25, 1415, Henry V's English army defeated a French army 3 times their size, largely thanks to the prowess of English archers. He was recognized as heir to the French throne but didn't live to fulfill that role (History.com Editors, 2010d).
41. **C. Mehmed I.** Though he only reigned for 8 years, Mehmed is remembered as being the restorer of the Ottoman empire, a major force on and around eastern Europe for centuries (Editors of Encyclopaedia Britannica, 2023b).
42. **A. The Holy Roman Empire.** The dukes of Saxony, starting with Otto I (r. 962–973), stepped in to fill the power vacuum left by the fall of the Carolingians. In the centuries that followed, the Holy Roman Emperor would be elected King of Germany and then, possibly, Holy Roman Emperor (Applied History Research Group, 1998).
43. **D. Robert the Bruce.** In order to finally grasp the crown of Scotland, Bruce killed his main rival, John "the Red" Comyn on the altar of a priory in Dumfries. The act was murder, treason, and blasphemy all at once, but it did have the desired effect (Solly, 2018).
44. **B. The Battle of Nicopolis.** Crusades had not been going well for the Christian armies in these late middle ages, and their crushing defeat at Nicopolis was largely down to the pride and arrogance of the French soldiers (Ciotola, 2013).
45. **A. Avignon.** The city was already owned by papal vassals, not, as some believed, by the French crown. Every pope and most of the cardinals elected during the Avignon Papacy (1309–1377) were, however, French. Pope Gregory XI returned the papacy to Rome, after much persuasion from saints Catherine of Siena and Bridget of Sweden. Rome wasn't happy to have him, and he might've moved back to Avignon again, if he hadn't died before he got the chance (Snell, 2020b).
46. **B. The Wars of the Roses.** The badge of Lancaster, the house of the ineffectual Henry VI and his determined queen Margaret of Anjou, was the red rose. The badge of York, house of Richard, Duke of York and his sons—two of whom became Edward IV and Richard III—was the white rose.

Questions

47. This statesman and author of *The Divine Comedy* was exiled from his beloved home city of Florence in 1302.
    a. Petrarch
    b. Plato
    c. Dante
    d. Bianchi
48. Though woodblock and metal movable type printing existed in China and Korea first, most historians credit this man with the invention of the printing press that ushered the Western world into the modern age.
    a. Johannes Gutenberg
    b. Thomas Edison
    c. Thomas Aquinus
    d. Eli Whitney
49. Though blast furnaces, which produced superior amounts of iron for steel, existed in China as early as the 5th century B.C., the oldest evidence of a blast furnace in Europe is from the 13th century in this country.
    a. England
    b. Sweden
    c. Russia
    d. France
50. These portable decorative elements, often made of wool but sometimes silk and gold as well, were the favorite decor of those who could afford them in the middle ages.
    a. Altars
    b. Chairs
    c. Tapestries
    d. Badges

Answers

47. **C. Dante.** Dante Alighieri, as part of his active political life, supported the cause of the *Bianchi* or "white" faction. When the opposing *Neri* or "black" faction gained power, he was exiled. He died in Ravenna without seeing Florence again (Falvey Library, 2019).
48. **A. Johannes Gutenberg.** Though Gutenberg himself died penniless, his invention revolutionized the way humans get and spread news and information, ushering in the modern age of humanity (Roos, 2019).
49. **B. Sweden.** The furnace excavated at Moshyttan in Sweden has been dated to 1250–1300, making Swedish metallurgists the frontrunners in new developments in European iron and steel (Myrstener et al., 2016).
50. **C. Tapestries.** These woven wall-hangings weren't just stylish additions to a bare stone room, but also served as insulation and protection from the elements (Cavallo, 1993).

Chapter 4:

Ancient American Splendor: Maya, Inca, and Aztec Empires

The Americas were home to many vibrant and powerful peoples long before contact with Europe brought them to the attention of the rest of the world. Their intricate societies developed based on the landscapes they inhabited, the political trials they faced, and the innovations they made in transportation and warfare. Three of the largest of these American empires were the Maya, the Inca, and the Aztec.

Astronomy, mathematics, architecture, agriculture—American peoples excelled at these fundamental sciences, achieving heights we're only just uncovering even today. So much of their history was either destroyed or disregarded by European colonizers, piecing it all together is an ongoing process. But it's important to remember that these people still exist, even if their empires are long gone; culturally, the Maya, Inca, and Aztec people are still very present in the indigenous peoples of their respective nations. They're doing the work to preserve and enrich their traditions, and by listening to them and learning about them, we can help.

Questions

1. The area of Mexico and Central America occupied by the Maya people before the Spanish conquistadors invaded is known as…
   a. The Panama Canal
   b. Mesoamerica
   c. South America
   d. Norteamericano
2. Aguada Fénix in Mexico, discovered with LiDAR mapping in 2020, is the oldest Mayan ruin we know of. It was built between…
   a. 1000–800 B.C.
   b. 3000–2000 B.C.
   c. 100–200 B.C.
   d. 300
3. Maya today speak 32 different languages, all descended from a Proto-Mayan tongue spoken some 4000 years ago in…
   a. Argentina
   b. Spain
   c. The United States of America
   d. Guatemala
4. This staple grain, along with beans, garden vegetables, and the occasional wild meat, was central to the diet in the Maya classic era (250–900) as well as today.
   a. Wheat
   b. Maize
   c. Rice
   d. Nuts
5. The Mayan Calendar consists of three separate, interlocking calendar wheels: the Tzolkin or divine calendar, the Haab or civil calendar, and this one that counts the years…
   a. Long Count
   b. Doomsday
   c. Frozen
   d. Fancy
6. This difficult-to-grow and complicated-to-process crop was central to ritual, social, and economic life for the Maya and the Olmecs before them.
   a. Tomatoes
   b. Saffron
   c. Cacao
   d. Pineapple
7. There was no centralized government in the Maya Empire; instead each city-state was ruled by its own…
   a. Oligarchy
   b. Monarchy
   c. Democracy
   d. Commune
8. This large city, a Mayan economic and political powerhouse, collapsed in the early 7th century, disrupting trade and communication all over the Mayan world.
   a. Teotihuacán
   b. Cuello
   c. Cush
   d. Nazca

Answers

1. **B. Mesoamerica.** The Mayan peoples lived in a large geographical block including parts of modern day Belize, Honduras, El Salvador, and Mexico–including all of the Yucatan peninsula–and all of Guatemala (History.com Editors, 2018w).
2. **A. 1000–800 B.C.** Aguada Fénix was finished in 800 but then, apparently, abandoned only 50 years later. This earliest known Maya ruin is different from later cities, in that it doesn't seem to have an administrative center but was more of a communal situation (Spray, 2023).
3. **D. Guatemala.** Although all Mayan languages are descendants of Proto-Mayan, modern-day speakers of Q'anjob'al, for example, would only understand modern K'iche' as well as an English speaker might understand German (UNC Libraries, 2012).
4. **B. Maize.** Though archaeologists have found that ancient Mayans had a varied and robust diet, maize or corn was always the central element, often grown in bulk while other vegetables came from kitchen gardens (Watson, 2017).
5. **A. Long Count.** Though the Long Count calendar predates the Mayan civilization, the Mayans used and made improvements to it. Long Count suggests a legendary creation date of August 11, 3114 B.C. There are multiple dates on which Long Count calendars "end," which signifies the end of an era and was a cause for great celebration (not the end of the world, as some people in 2012 thought) (Borowski, 2012).
6. **C. Cacao.** Cacao trees have very specific requirements for growth, so they took just-so conditions and a great deal of knowledge to cultivate. The pods are then fermented, dried, and roasted, and whole families or communities would get together to process them socially (Garthwaite, 2015).
7. **B. Monarchy.** Classic Mayan city-states had hereditary kings who were believed to have a personal connection to the divine. This gave them the authority to mediate between the natural and supernatural worlds for their people (Mayan Civilization, 2019).
8. **A. Teotihuacán.** As the largest and most populous city in Mesoamerica, when Teotihuacán fell, it left a massive political void that sped the decline of Mayan civilization (Mayan Civilization, 2019).

Questions

9. These domesticated animals were imported and then eventually bred by Maya peoples as early as 300 B.C.–100.
    a. Highland cattle
    b. Turkeys
    c. Silkworms
    d. Poodles
10. This beautiful pigment remains bright on many Maya objects, regardless of weather and centuries of wear.
    a. Maya blue
    b. Maya green
    c. Copper
    d. Gold Flake
11. This civic structure was central to Mayan social, religious, and even political life.
    a. The arena
    b. The fountain
    c. The circus
    d. The ballcourt
12. The Maya used this concept as a placeholder when writing numbers, making it one of the earliest recorded uses of the concept in the world.
    a. X
    b. Zero
    c. Negatives
    d. Imaginary Numbers
13. Maya peoples in the ancient Americas referred to themselves by the names of their city-states; the word "Maya" came to have an overarching meaning only after…
    a. 1000 B.C.
    b. 1776
    c. 1524
    d. 2013
14. Maya peoples wrote many books on varied topics such as astronomy, mathematics, spirituality, and mythology. Sadly, only four of all of them remain today, known as…
    a. Codices
    b. Bibles
    c. Libros
    d. Translations
15. Spanish invaders like Cortés brought this deadly disease to the Maya after first giving it to the Aztecs and nearly decimating their population.
    a. Chicken pox
    b. COVID-19
    c. Smallpox
    d. Polio
16. These mythical creatures, considered to be the first prehistoric people to occupy the Yucatan and protectors of her natural features to this day, are central to Mayan spirituality.
    a. Aluxes
    b. Goblins
    c. Fairies
    d. Golems

Answers

9. **B. Turkeys.** The bones of domesticated Mexican turkeys (as opposed to the native, wild turkeys) have been found in Mayan archaeological sites in Guatemala. They may have been used as food and sacrifices. All domestic turkeys today are descended from this species (Torrent, 2012).
10. **A. Maya blue.** A clear, sky blue, this pigment was made by heating indigo and palygorskite, a mineral found in local clay. It seemed almost impervious to wear and tear, when it was given time to set properly (Chang, 2008).
11. **D. The ballcourt.** The Mayan ball game of *pitz* was used to settle disputes, choose sacrifices, honor the gods, and even to entertain. It's even central to some of their myths, especially those of the Maize Gods and the Hero Twins (Hudson Museum, 2013).
12. **B. Zero.** Mayan writing used zero as a placeholder when writing numbers, rather than it being a symbol for "nothing." It was often drawn to look like a seashell (West, 2019).
13. **C. 1524.** "Maya" as an umbrella term for a widespread people didn't come into use until the Spanish began invading. In spite of attempts by colonizers, Maya culture is still varied, alive, and vibrant today (Tuyuc, 2022).
14. **A. Codices.** Many of these information-packed books, painted on paper made of fig tree bark, were burned by Fray Diego de Landa, a priest who'd spent 13 years getting to know the Maya people, culture, and even language, in 1562. Only four are known to survive (Yucatan Times, 2021).
15. **C. Smallpox.** The conquistadors from Spain conquered much faster thanks to smallpox, to which the Maya and other indigenous Americans had no natural immunity (NIH, 2020).
16. **A. Aluxes.** Even today, it's considered possible to connect to Aluxes on one's own land with the help of a shaman, and ask them for help and guidance (Cervera, 2022).

Questions

17. The great Maya Pyramid of Uxmal is also known as the Pyramid of the Magician or the Pyramid of the…
    a. Best friends
    b. Fish
    c. Dwarf
    d. Elf
18. While the Maya revered many trees as sacred, medicinal, or food sources, this one represented the universe and the connection between the underworld, the human world, and the heavens.
    a. Oak
    b. Ceiba
    c. Ash
    d. Juniper
19. In the Aztec mythos, they migrated from the north, where they lived in an undying land called…
    a. Isla
    b. Aztlan
    c. Tenochtitlan
    d. Huitzilopochtli
20. The Aztec people called themselves this.
    a. Mexica
    b. Toltec
    c. Chichimeca
    d. Ilhuicamina
21. This Aztec language is still spoken by millions of people in modern-day Mexico.
    a. Spanish
    b. K'iche'
    c. Nahuatl
    d. Quechua
22. These marvels of Aztec agricultural technology are a kind of floating raised bed still used today in Mexico.
    a. Chinampas
    b. Rice Paddies
    c. Aqueducts
    d. Hydroponics
23. Aztecs settled this city, their largest and greatest, on the swampy borders of Lake Texcoco in 1325.
    a. Oaxaca
    b. Xochimilco
    c. Tepaneca
    d. Tenochtitlán
24. This great Aztec leader formed the triple alliance between his city of Tenochtitlán, Tlacopan, Texcoco to become the dominant force in 1426.
    a. Itzcoatl
    b. Metzli
    c. Ixtli
    d. Atzi

Answers

17. **C. Dwarf.** A famous Maya story recorded in the 19th century tells of a small man born from an egg raised by a witch of Uxmal. Through his mother's magic, the dwarf bested the governor of Uxmal in three contests, one of which involved the great pyramid (Smithsonian Institute, n.d.b).
18. **B. Ceiba.** It's said that the Maya gods planted ceiba trees in the four directions of the cosmos, and then the one in the center that linked the three cosmic realms (Yucatan Today, 2014).
19. **B. Aztlan.** The name means "the white land" or "land of the heron," and was a paradise of plenty where they had everything, until they wandered away (Maistri, 2019).
20. **A. Mexica.** The Mexica's mythic origin story claims they left their perfect home and braved many years of dangerous wandering before they founded their first great city (Maistri, 2019).
21. **C. Nahuatl.** Another element of the Aztec origin myth is that there were seven Nahuatl-speaking tribes, of which the Mexica were the last to arrive in modern-day Mexico (Schmal, 2020).
22. **A. Chinampas.** These Aztec floating gardens are still made by criss crossing layers of mud and compost—or compost-to-be. The oldest ones in Mexico go back as far as 1250 (Hirst, 2019).
23. **D. Tenochtitlán.** In order to build there, the Aztecs had to drain the swamps and construct artificial islands for agriculture and building foundations (History.com Editors, 2009b).
24. **A. Itzcoatl.** Itzcoatl or "obsidian snake" and his coalition of weakest-link city-states banded together to take advantage of a power vacuum in the then-dominant Azcapotzalco. After they won, Tenochtitlán was the center of Aztec power (Roos, 2021).

Questions

25. Unlike most wars, this Aztec conflict involved highly ritualized single combat and was probably meant to placate the gods and provide captives for sacrifice.
    a. Mexican Civil War
    b. Spanish-American War
    c. Flower War
    d. Nahuatl War
26. In battle, Aztec warriors had the ultimate goal of…
    a. Killing their enemies
    b. Capturing their enemies
    c. Raiding towns
    d. Burning down forests
27. When an Aztec army conquered a new city-state, they mostly left the politicians and leaders in place, instead demanding…
    a. A feast
    b. Prisoners
    c. Regular tribute
    d. A written apology
28. Ruins of Tenochtitlán still exist in this modern-day city, including those of the Great Temple.
    a. Mexico City
    b. Oaxaca
    c. Tijuana
    d. Guadalajara
29. Aztec civilization relied on water and this for transport of goods and people.
    a. Llamas
    b. Horses
    c. Oxen
    d. Humans
30. This "feathered serpent" god existed in Mesoamerica as early as the ancient Olmecs (1200–400 B.C.) and was deeply important to the Aztecs.
    a. Chichen Itza
    b. Quetzalcoatl
    c. Itzcoatl
    d. Calimoxo
31. This last independent ruler of the Aztec Empire was a rich, admired, intelligent, and successful expansionist.
    a. Cesar
    b. Tezcatlipoca
    c. Xochicalco
    d. Montezuma II
32. The Aztec civilization maintained power over the Valley of Mexico between 1325 and…
    a. 1521
    b. 1602
    c. 1066
    d. 1920

Answers

25. **C. Flower War.** The Flower War, Flowery War, or *xochicayotl* is a matter of much debate among scholars. It seems clear, however, that this was a series of single combats for honor rather than a war of expansion and domination (Pennock, 2022).
26. **B. Capturing enemies.** Though the first captive was often sacrificed on the battlefield, most captives were taken home to be sacrificed in thanks to the gods. This was believed to be a necessary part of keeping their cities healthy and happy (Pennock, 2022).
27. **C. Regular tribute.** Rather than replacing the entire political community structure, Aztec kings simply required that conquered city-states and territories send luxuries and other tribute goods—taxation, effectively (Pennock, 2022).
28. **A. Mexico City.** As it was during the reign of the Aztec Empire, Mexico City is the most populous city in Mexico today. Though conquistadors built the modern city on the ruins of the great Aztec city, today archaeologists are unearthing its rich past (Alex, 2018).
29. **D. Humans.** Without the wheel or domesticated pack animals, Aztec civilization built towering temples, complex cities, aqueducts, and an entire empire. It was all on the strength of human power (Meyer & Willey, 2018).
30. **B. Quetzalcoatl.** Though Quetzalcoatl may not have started off as a god—in fact, he may be based on the founder of the earlier Toltec civilization, Ce Acatl Topiltzín Quetzalcoatl—his cult was widespread by the year 900 (Minster, 2023).
31. **D. Montezuma II.** Cortés, the Spanish Conquistador who made first contact with Montezuma II, later made it sound as if he practically handed his empire over to Cortés, and therefore King Charles V of Spain, when he needed to flatter the king. In fact, far from thinking the Spanish were gods or sent by the gods, Montezuma II was curious about them and keen to discover who they were. The conquistadors took advantage of this curiosity (Roos, 2020).
32. **A. 1521.** After years of bloody war with Cortés and his men, Tenochtitlán finally fell—a feat the Spanish couldn't have accomplished without the collaboration of the Tlaxcaltec (Roos, 2020).

Questions

33. These Nahuatl "song-dances" transmitted Aztec culture and lore down through the generations long before they were collected by colonizing Spaniards.
    a. Carnavals
    b. Cuicatl
    c. Chansons
    d. Chants
34. This legendary Inca founder is sometimes said to have led his 4 sisters and 3 brothers to bring civilization and technology to modern-day Cusco.
    a. Manco Cápac
    b. Tintin
    c. Ayacucho
    d. Guaman Poma
35. Another Inca foundation myth says the founder and one of his sisters emerged from this massive lake before making their way to Cusco.
    a. Lake Victoria
    b. Lake Huron
    c. Lake Titicaca
    d. Mar Chiquita
36. This Inca name for their own empire, once it was established, meant "the four regions."
    a. Cusco
    b. Tawantinsuyu
    c. Ecuador
    d. Andes
37. This mountain range, the highest in the Americas and the longest in the world, shaped the Inca empire dramatically.
    a. The Rockies
    b. The Himalayas
    c. The Alps
    d. The Andes
38. This language, while just one of many used in Inca-ruled lands, served as the empire's *lingua franca.*
    a. Diné
    b. Quechua
    c. Tagalog
    d. Yaqui
39. This pre-Incan civilization in Peru is best known for its monumental geoglyphs, etched into the earth and only visible from far above.
    a. Nazca
    b. Hopi
    c. Chaldean
    d. Portuguese
40. This ingenious invention allowed Inca people to record amounts and numbers via a system of cords and knots.
    a. Wheels
    b. Quipu
    c. Bracelets
    d. Quinoa

Answers

33. **B. Cuicatl.** These poems speak of affection, friendship, beauty, and heroic feats. Next to prowess in warfare, the composing of *cuicatl* was the most highly prized skill in Aztec culture (Szoblik, 2020).
34. **A. Manco Cápac.** Manco is said to have taught the Hualla people living in what would become Cusco about agriculture; one of his sisters taught them about weaving (Welford, 2022).
35. **C. Lake Titicaca.** The largest lake in South America, and also one of the highest at 12,500 feet above sea level, Lake Titicaca looms large in Inca mythology and history (Machicao, 2023).
36. **B. Tawantinsuyu.** The four regions were Antisuyu, Contisuyu, Chinchaysuyu, and Collasuyu, all of which had different resources to contribute to the empire ruled from Cusco in the very center (Smithsonian Institute, 2014).
37. **D. The Andes.** Due to the particular challenges the Andes presented, the Inca developed marvelous feats of engineering, such as their terraced agriculture, 15,000 miles of roads, and monumental architecture (History.com Editors, 2014).
38. **B. Quechua.** Called Runa by its native speakers in the Andes, this Inca language is spoken by over 8 million people today (Penn Language Center, 2015).
39. **A. Nazca.** The Nazca culture existed in Peru between 100 B.C. and 700. Though many theories have been put forward, no one knows definitively what purpose the huge drawings served (History.com Editors, 2018e).
40. **B. Quipu.** A long, llama-wool cord with a series of pendant cords attached to it, the quipu made mathematical information easily—and accurately—portable (Swetz, 2008).

Questions

41. The Inca royal family was considered semi-divine, since they were descended directly from this sun god.
    a. Atahualpa
    b. Apollo
    c. Inti
    d. Sol
42. Inca, though now used as a catch-all for the peoples of the Inca Empire, specifically refers to the noble class, including the *Sapa Inca* or…
    a. King or Emperor
    b. Conquistador
    c. Revolutionary
    d. Prime Minister
43. Key to the success of the Inca empire, these mammals were the only domesticated pack animal in the ancient Americas.
    a. Mules
    b. Llamas
    c. Emus
    d. Camels
44. Perhaps the most famous Sapa Inca, Pachacuti, conquered, organized, and arranged most of the empire himself, as well as possibly building this magnificent Inca site.
    a. Quito
    b. Angkor Wat
    c. Intihuatana
    d. Machu Picchu
45. Above all other animals, the Inca revered the puma, the snake, and this massive bird, thought to be able to deliver messages between the earthly realm and the heavenly realm.
    a. Bald Eagle
    b. Condor
    c. Hawk
    d. Vulture
46. At its high point in the early 1500s, the Inca Empire included modern-day Peru, a large swathe of Chile, and parts of…
    a. Brazil
    b. Uruguay and Argentina
    c. Bolivia, Ecuador, and Colombia
    d. Panama and Costa Rica
47. *Sapa Incas* and other nobles often received this treatment after death.
    a. Burial at sea
    b. Cremation
    c. Beheading
    d. Mummification
48. This luxury textile could only be worn and used by the highest echelons of Inca society.
    a. Wool
    b. Cumbi
    c. Tunic
    d. Andes

Answers

41. **C. Inti.** He was one of the most important gods in the Inca pantheon; the progress of the sun was carefully marked by the people, who celebrated solstices and equinoxes and were disturbed by eclipses (Minster, 2020).
42. **A. King or Emperor.** Between 1198 and 1593, there were 13 *Sapa Inca*, chosen by the man before them from among his sons or close family (Discover Peru.org, 2019).
43. **B. Llamas.** They weren't just the only pack animals going—llamas also provided excellent wool for textiles and technologies that kept the empire going (PBS, 2005).
44. **D. Machu Picchu.** Though it was rediscovered by the rest of the world in 1911, no one is entirely sure if this breathtaking site functioned as a noble estate, a religious complex, a trade hub, or something else entirely (History.com Editors, 2011).
45. **B. Condor.** This majestic bird was the go-between for the gods, often thought immortal. It's part of the sacred Inca Trilogy, with the puma and snake, all three of which are repeating themes in Inca art and architecture (Machaca, n.d.).
46. **C. Bolivia, Ecuador, and Colombia.** The conquests of Sapa Inca Huayna Capac brought the Inca empire all the way to the Ancasmayo River (History.com Editors, 2015).
47. **D. Mummification.** At festivals and sacred occasions, the mummies of past *sapa incas* would be taken out, paraded for the public, and revered by the people as objects of worship (History.com Editors, 2015).
48. **B. Cumbi.** The weaving and design of *cumbi* fabric was highly regulated by Inca officials. Only certain very skilled men and women were permitted to weave it (McHugh, 2020).

Questions

49. Inca peoples made many useful medical discoveries, including this leaf that acts as a painkiller and energy-booster.
    a. Sassafras
    b. Ginkgo
    c. Coca
    d. Willow
50. Imported diseases and a war of succession between Huáscar and this last independent *Sapa Inca* had weakened the empire by the time Spain invaded Cusco in earnest.
    a. Montezuma
    b. Atahualpa
    c. Viracocha
    d. Manco Cápac

Answers

49. **C. Coca.** At first, Spanish conquistadors tried to stamp out Inca use of the coca plant, whether for medical or religious reasons. Later, they decided to exploit it as a cash crop (Biondich & Joslin, 2016).
50. **B. Atahualpa.** Francisco Pizarro took advantage of his accidentally good timing and captured Atahualpa, eventually killing him in 1533 (History.com Editors, 2019c).

Chapter 5:

Standing on the Shoulders of Giants: The Renaissance

The Renaissance is usually dated from the 15th century in Europe, although stirrings of the progressive thinking that characterized it were present as early as the 13th century in some ways, well into the Middle Ages. Although Classical texts were alive and well in other societies, it was during the Renaissance that western Europe rediscovered them. Philosophy, religion, rhetoric, and human expression of all kinds were forever changed by this focus on the thinkers of the past.

The Renaissance was multifaceted, a rethinking of religious, philosophical, political, and economic values for the world at large.

Feudalism wasn't cutting it anymore, especially as the general populace became more literate and books became more accessible. While the rich patronized visual art, literature, and music in the middle ages, money poured into artistic pursuits like never before during the Renaissance. Families with enough money, be they noble or otherwise, could patronize artists. This became another metric by which to measure reputation and honor. While this mode of thinking looked backward, it was also startlingly progressive after the strictures of society in the Middle Ages; social mobility became marginally more possible and craftspeople and merchants gained a voice in their own government once again.

All of these changes didn't come easily, of course. The Catholic Church, a bastion of authority during the Middle Ages, came under fire from the Protestant Reformation that spread out from Germany. While God's authority was rarely questioned yet, the Pope's most certainly was during the Renaissance, as Europe questioned the place and the limits of humanity. Rulers felt themselves subject to their people for the first time, in many cases, in a lasting and continuous way, instead of just the other way around. It was a time of great genius and innovation but also a time of massive upheaval and unrest. Let's jump into the Renaissance.

Questions

1. *Renaissance* is a French word meaning this.
    a. Revolution
    b. Rebirth
    c. Astrology
    d. Music
2. Since Renaissance ideas spread out from Italy slowly at first, there's a lot of overlap with the culture of this previous period of European history and that of the Renaissance.
    a. Georgian
    b. Napoleonic
    c. The Middle Ages
    d. Rococo
3. This intellectual movement both inaugurated and dominated Renaissance thought in Western Europe from as early as the 13th century.
    a. Humanism
    b. Communism
    c. Spiritualism
    d. Ludditism
4. Lorenzo Ghiberti's relief carvings on the doors of the Baptistery of this Italian city's cathedral of Santa Maria del Fiore are one of the first works to completely embody Renaissance ideals of art.
    a. Venice
    b. Porto
    c. Florence
    d. Rome
5. The cathedral of Santa Maria del Fiore boasts the largest masonry dome in existence even today, designed and constructed by Filippo Brunelleschi with the patronage of this wealthy Italian banking family.
    a. Borgia
    b. Medici
    c. Cavalcanti
    d. Alighieri
6. Writing in the Italian vernacular instead of Latin, this poet is often credited with revolutionizing literature in the Renaissance.
    a. Petrarch
    b. Cervantes
    c. Malory
    d. Pazzi
7. Fillipo Brunelleschi and this Renaissance artist are credited with rediscovering and codifying linear perspective, a technique for depicting space on two-dimensional surfaces like walls, wood, and canvas.
    a. Frank Llyod Wright
    b. I. M. Pei
    c. Dante
    d. Leon Battista Alberti
8. This traveling Dutch scholar of the early 1500s often took the Catholic Church of the time to task for corruption and advocated a return to simpler Christianity.
    a. Van Eyck
    b. Erasmus
    c. Da Vinci
    d. Van Gogh

Answers

1. **B. Rebirth.** Starting in Italy in the 14th century, philosophers, artists, scientists, and thinkers of all kinds began to rediscover Classical ideas that had been out of favor in Europe in the Middle Ages—if not forgotten altogether in that part of the world. The Renaissance saw these ideas reborn (The Editors of Encyclopedia Britannica, 2018c).
2. **C. The Middle Ages.** Often called "the Dark Ages" because scholars during the Renaissance looked back and saw that Classical ideas had all-but-disappeared in Western Europe during those years (The Editors of Encyclopedia Britannica, 2018c).
3. **A. Humanism.** Renaissance Humanism looked to Classical Greek and Latin texts for cues about how to live and work in the world, especially in terms of morality. The idea was that humans made the world what it was, and we were capable of making it better. This was a huge shift from the religion-based thinking of the Middle Ages (Wilde, 2023).
4. **C. Florence.** The Calimala, a wealthy wool-merchants' guild in Florence, sponsored a contest to decorate the Baptistery doors. The two finalist entries were those of Filippo Brunelleschi, who designed the cathedral's engineering masterpiece, its dome, and Ghiberti, who ultimately won (Lubow, 2007).
5. **B. Medici.** Originally a humble family of wool merchants, the Medici experienced intense pushback from families of Florentine nobility as they rose to influence in the city and its governing body, the *signoria*. Lorenzo de Medici, called "the Magnificent" patronized and championed artists and thinkers like Botticelli, da Vinci, Michelangelo, and Donatello while running his family, their bank, and much of the city from the late 1400s (Opera Magazine, 2020).
6. **A. Petrarch.** Francesco Petrarca's work, especially his vivid descriptions, blurred the lines between the visual arts and the literary, as well as inspiring a great deal of both (Bruhns, 2017).
7. **D. Leon Battista Alberti.** While Brunelleschi is credited with rediscovering perspective from Classical sources, Alberti was the first to publish a coherent theory of perspective in his 1435 treatise *Della Pictura* or *On Painting* (Lienau, 2013).
8. **B. Erasmus.** Through his travels and studies, Erasmus—or Gerrit Gerritszoon—was part of a lively network of scholars and thinkers that bounced ideas off each other and elevated Renaissance Humanism to new heights (BBC History, 2014).

Questions

9. This sculptor's *David*, a bronze commissioned by Cosimo de Medici for his Palazzo, shows a beautiful youth rather than the large, muscled figure often depicted by artists of the time.
    a. Donatello
    b. Botticelli
    c. Bach
    d. Dürer
10. This artist, scientist, and military engineer left thousands of notebook pages full of writing and drawing—with much of it mirror handwriting, since he was left-handed and found it easier to work this way.
    a. Michelangelo
    b. Caravaggio
    c. Da Vinci
    d. Raphael
11. This Pope-friendly document was faked sometime between 750–800 and unmasked as a forgery by a Renaissance Humanist called Valla in 1440.
    a. The Declaration of the Rights of Man
    b. The Donation of Constantine
    c. The Papal Bulls
    d. The *Vox Populi*
12. On October 31, 1517, this man published his *95 Theses* (aka *Disputation on the Power of Indulgences*) in Wittenburg, setting the Protestant Reformation in motion.
    a. Henry VIII
    b. Charles V
    c. Martin Luther
    d. John Calvin
13. Constantinople, the glory of the Eastern Roman Empire, fell to this empire on May 29, 1453.
    a. Mongol
    b. Chola
    c. Maya
    d. Ottoman
14. This Dominican friar famously railed at the corruption of the papacy and the worldliness of the Florentine upper classes—he was also responsible for the Bonfire of the Vanities on 7 February 1497.
    a. Savonarola
    b. Benedict
    c. Augustine
    d. Brutus
15. This Italian Renaissance Mathematician and monk worked, traveled, and lived with Leonardo Da Vinci for a time all over Italy.
    a. Luca Pacioli
    b. Isaac Newton
    c. Euclid
    d. Ludovica Sforza

Answers

9. **A. Donatello.** The sculpture, which depicts David as a triumphant boy, was considered scandalous in later years for its complete nudity (a Classical-period callback) and its almost androgynous beauty, accented by the elegant Renaissance-favorite *contrapposto* stance David takes. Florentines of the time, on the other hand, seem to have loved the statue (Meyer, 2022).
10. **C. Da Vinci.** Leonardo Da Vinci, born in the Italian town of Vinci, near Florence, worked for the Medici there, the Sforzas in Milan, Pope Leo X in Rome, and finally Francis I of France. While he had trouble finishing painting commissions—he left many undone when he died—his mind was constantly on the move, learning, researching, and exploring new artistic and scientific frontiers (Amsen, 2019).
11. **B. The Donation of Constantine.** This medieval forgery granted the Pope supreme religious rulership over much of Christendom, including Constantinople, as if decreed by the Emperor Constantine himself. Valla's debunking of this document led, in many ways, to the Protestant Reformation (Wilde, 2020).
12. **C. Martin Luther.** In his *Theses*, Luther challenged many time-honored dictates of the Catholic Church, who'd held religious domination over Western Europe for centuries. He particularly disliked that the Church allowed people to buy indulgences, or papers of forgiveness, for their sins (Wilkinson, 2022).
13. **D. Ottoman.** Sultan Mehmed II besieged Constantinople for 55 days before finally breaching the walls. Without its protection, the Byzantine Empire crumbled quickly (Hudson, 2018).
14. **A. Savonarola.** Fra Girolamo Savonarola's fiery sermons stirred Florentines up to a fever pitch. He convinced many of them to burn their "vanities," things such as art, makeup, mirrors, and fancy clothing. He was eventually defrocked and executed by the Church itself (Eschner, 2017).
15. **A. Luca Pacioli.** Pacioli's most famous works are *Summa de arithmetica, geometria, proportioni et proportionalita* and *Divina proportione*, the latter of which was illustrated by Da Vinci (O'Connor & Robertson, 2020).

Questions

16. This Pope, born Giuliano della Rovere, is best known for his close and sometimes contentious relationship with Michelangelo, from whom he commissioned the frescoes on the Sistine Chapel ceiling, for engaging Raphael to paint his frescoes at the Vatican, and for conceiving the idea for a new St. Peter's Basilica.
    a. Alexander VI
    b. Pope Julius II
    c. John Paul II
    d. Innocent III
17. On 6 May 1527, this King of Spain and Holy Roman Empire sacked Rome and forced Pope Clement VII—who'd been fighting him for power for years—to compromise with him.
    a. Phillip II
    b. Ferdinand II
    c. Charles V
    d. Maximillian I
18. This Florentine statesman is best known today for his seminal book of strategy, *The Prince*, which has made his name a synonym for calculating political operators.
    a. Dante Alighieri
    b. Niccolo Machiavelli
    c. Petrarch
    d. Giovanni Bocaccio
19. This Marchioness of Mantua negotiated her husband's release when he was captured by Charles VIII of France, ruled Mantua as her son's regent until he came of age, and defended her own property and home under siege.
    a. Julia Farnese
    b. Isabella d'Este
    c. Clarice Orsini
    d. Caterina de Medici
20. This daughter of Pope Alexander VI had a (probably undeserved) scandalous reputation thanks to her corrupt father and brutal brother, but eventually became a successful and respected Duchess of Ferrara.
    a. Lucrezia Borgia
    b. Julia Farnese
    c. Contessina de Bardi
    d. Ginevra di benci
21. This French Protestant settled in Geneva, where he spread his doctrine of predestination and helped to create a culture of strict, state-enforced morality.
    a. Martin Luther
    b. John Wesley
    c. Pius XII
    d. John Calvin
22. Though it began in the Middle Ages, this office within the Catholic Church developed a particularly nasty reputation during the Renaissance in Spain under Tomas de Torquemada.
    a. The Inquisition
    b. The Office of Official Secrets
    c. The College of Cardinals
    d. The Exorcist

Answers

16. **B. Julius II.** This pope, who'd survived at least one assassination attempt during the rule of his predecessor Alexander VI, was a politically savvy player who not only patronized the arts but took it upon himself to restore the Papal States (Kühner, 2020).
17. **C. Charles V.** A member of the long-ruling Habsburg Dynasty, Charles struggled with both his own Catholic Church and the growing Protestant Reformation throughout his rule. He eventually abdicated and retired to a monastery at Yuste (de Ferdinandy, 2019).
18. **B. Niccolo Machiavelli.** *The Prince* was only published in 1532, after his death. It's been popular but controversial, and on many banned books lists, ever since. While his name is a synonym for deviousness to many people, in fact *The Prince* is more about pragmatism in good rule, not greed and cruelty masked by subterfuge (History.com Editors, 2018m).
19. **B. Isabella d'Este.** She was also a great beauty who was friends with many Renaissance painters and scholars. She had her portrait painted by Da Vinci and Titian among others (Lewis, 2019b).
20. **A. Lucrezia Borgia.** Many contemporary tales accusing her of everything from adultery to murder have been told since her father was elected to the Papacy, but she ended her days in a convent, long after her father and brother had died. To this day, her name is a byword for a murderous woman—particularly one suspected of poisoning (Biography.com Editors, 2021).

21. **D. John Calvin.** Calvinists developed a reputation for hard work largely because they weren't allowed to do much else. Feasting, dancing, singing, attending the theater, drinking, gambling, games, dressing too fancy, disrespect, even naming children anything not appearing in the Old Testament, were proscribed (Hicks, 2013).
22. **A. The Inquisition.** Created to seek out and end Heresy both within the Catholic Church and without, the Inquisition went after Jews, "Witches," Protestants, Muslims, and Indigenous People, among others, all over the world. Today, it exists in a much milder form as The Congregation for the Doctrine of the Faith (History.com Editors, 2017b).

Questions

23. This Renaissance King was a patron of the arts, an eventual proponent of the Reformation, and an excellent athlete and hunter—but he's best remembered as the English King who went through six different wives.
    a. James I
    b. William the Conqueror
    c. Henry VIII
    d. Charles I
24. This Catholic English queen inherited the throne on the death of her Protestant brother, Edward VI, in spite of a Protestant plot to install a cousin, Lady Jane Grey, on the throne in 1553.
    a. Elizabeth II
    b. Matilda
    c. Victoria
    d. Mary I
25. During Henry VIII's rule, this Archbishop of Canterbury, a seminal voice in the English Reformation, was rumored to have a secret wife who traveled all over the country with him… in a box.
    a. Thomas Cranmer
    b. Thomas More
    c. Oliver Cromwell
    d. Thomas Becket
26. This artist brought the artistic principles of the Renaissance from Italy to Germany, becoming the best known German artist of the era.
    a. Pablo Picasso
    b. Albrecht Dürer
    c. Max Ernst
    d. Otto Mueller
27. This revolutionary thinker and physician is credited with introducing more chemistry to the medical profession—though he would've called himself an alchemist.
    a. Hermes
    b. Hippocrates
    c. Paracelsus
    d. Galen
28. This Polish astronomer developed his heliocentric theory of the solar system as early as 1508, but it wasn't fully realized until he published his *De revolutionibus orbium coelestium libri vi* or "Six Books Concerning the Revolutions of the Heavenly Orbs" in 1543.
    a. Nicolaus Copernicus
    b. Archimedes
    c. Domenico Maria de Novara
    d. Claudius Ptolemy
29. These French Protestants represented as much as 8% of the total population of France in the 16th century, the peak of their political influence.
    a. Dominicans
    b. Huguenots
    c. Refugees
    d. Methodists

Answers

23. **C. Henry VIII.** This king famously changed England's state religion from Catholicism to the protestant Church of England when the Pope wouldn't let him divorce his first wife, Catherine of Aragon, and marry someone else. Anne Boleyn, the wife he decided on, was instrumental in bringing protestant ideology into play in England. She was eventually beheaded on trumped-up charges of adultery.
24. **D. Mary I.** Later known as "Bloody Mary" for her burning of Protestants, Mary ruled England in her own right as the daughter of Henry VIII. All this in spite of the Jane Grey plot, her male advisors trying to use her power to their own advantage, and her marriage to the King of Spain, Phillip II, which was unpopular with the English people (Solly, 2020).
25. **A. Thomas Cranmer.** Though there's no real evidence, only stories of Mrs. Cranmer's box, it is a fact that Cranmer married his wife Margarete while on diplomatic service for Henry VIII and brought her back with him when he was called to the Archbishopric by his king. At the time, English clergy weren't allowed to marry yet (Staats, 2014).
26. **B. Dürer.** In August of 1494, plague broke out in Dürer's home city of Nuremberg, where he had been working as an artist and designer. He left and traveled over the Alps to Italy, where he got to know many Renaissance artists and their methods (Hand 2018).
27. **C. Paracelsus.** Theophrastus Philippus Aureolus Bombastus von Hohenheim, or Paracelsus as he's better known, is also the source of the word "bombastic." His ideas were revolutionary, but his writings show no sign of hesitation in claiming his correctness (Goodrick-Clarke, n.d.).
28. **A. Nicolaus Copernicus.** Copernicus gave credit to his predecessor astronomers like Ptolemy, saying that he'd simply ordered the parts they'd discovered and placed together somewhat chaotically (Editors of Encyclopaedia Britannica, 2019d).
29. **B. Huguenots.** It's unclear where the term Huguenot came from, only that at one time it was used by French Catholics as an insult. Sometime in the 18th century it was reclaimed by people of Huguenot ancestry as a cultural label.

Questions

30. Luís Vaz de Camões wrote lyric, epic, and dramatic poetry that's considered seminal literature of this, his home country, to this day.
    a. Brasil
    b. Spain
    c. Kenya
    d. Portugal
31. This playwright delighted Londoners with histories like *Henry V*, tragedies like *Hamlet*, and comedies like *Much Ado About Nothing.*
    a. Christopher Marlowe
    b. Thomas Malory
    c. William Shakespeare
    d. Robert Frost
32. This Flemish painter and engraver is most famous for his scenes of raucous peasant life such as in *Kermis* and *The Peasant Wedding.*
    a. Pieter Brueghel
    b. Rembrandt van Rijn
    c. Francisco de Goya
    d. Vincent van Gogh
33. This seminal Spanish author was a courageous navy veteran, held captive by Barbary Pirates for five years before being ransomed back to Madrid. It was many years before he saw literary success with *Don Quixote.*
    a. Hamlet
    b. Miguel de Cervantes
    c. Sancho Panza
    d. Lope de Vega
34. Though it blends with other surrounding time periods, the European Renaissance is considered to be loosely…
    a. 12th–13th centuries
    b. 14th–17th centuries
    c. 18th–20th centuries
    d. 19th–21st centuries
35. This Northern Renaissance painter is most famous for his *Ghent Altarpiece* and the clever-yet-somber *Arnolfini Portrait*, which features an enigmatic concave mirror in the background.
    a. Rogier van der Weyden
    b. Robert Campin
    c. Titian
    d. Jan van Eyck
36. This economic theory, which focuses on maximizing exports while minimizing imports, was favored in many Renaissance European countries.
    a. Socialism
    b. Game Theory
    c. Mercantilism
    d. The Principle of Self-Interest
37. This Italian-born Queen of France developed an unfortunate reputation long before her involvement with the St. Bartholomew's Day massacre of 1572.
    a. Joan of Arc
    b. Catherine de Medici
    c. Kathryn Howard
    d. Mary Stuart

Answers

30. **D. Portugal.** In his epic poem, *Os Lusíadas*, Camões immortalizes navigator Vasco de Gama's discovery of a sea route to India. It invokes the Classical gods as witnesses to, helpers of, and even obstacles to de Gama's trials (Editors of Encyclopedia Britannica, 2023).
31. **C. William Shakespeare.** Born in Stratford-Upon-Avon in 1564 the son of a merchant and bailiff, Shakespeare appeared suddenly as a playwright in London in the 1590s. We know remarkably little about his personal life, for such a popular figure (History.com Editors, 2019a).
32. **A. Pieter Brueghel.** Though not of peasant birth himself, Brueghel's interest in complex compositions of country activity earned him the nickname "Peasant Brueghel" (Wisse, 2019).
33. **B. Miguel de Cervantes.** He also worked as a requisitions officer for the Spanish Armada and a decent-but-not-famous playwright before *Don Quixote Part I* was published in 1605. *Part II* appeared in 1615 (Reilly, n.d.).
34. **B. 14th–17th centuries.** Many early developments before the full flower of the Renaissance, like the printing press, were technically in the middle ages, but get lumped in due to the cultural significance to the Renaissance and its values (History.com Editors, 2018c).
35. **D. Jan van Eyck.** Well known for his incredible attention to minute detail, it's often been suggested that van Eyck put himself in the concave mirror–and that you, the viewer, are the other figure in it (Al-Sharif, 2019).
36. **C. Mercantilism.** Collecting as many resources and as much wealth over the world, under this theory, would lead to being stronger and better positioned than any competing nations (MasterClass, 2022).
37. **B. Catherine de Medici.** Queen, regent, and queen mother at different times during the stressful French Civil Wars of Religion, Catherine spent most of her time trying to calm the warring Guise (Catholic) and Bourbon (Protestant) factions at court (Solly, 2022).

Questions

38. This artist's 14 foot tall *David* was installed in the Piazza della Signoria in Florence, the heart of the city's political and artistic life, in 1504.
    a. Da Vinci
    b. Botticelli
    c. Rodin
    d. Michelangelo
39. The third and last of Henry VIII's children to rule England, this monarch refused to marry, claiming to be married to England itself.
    a. Elizabeth I
    b. Mary Stuart
    c. James Stuart
    d. Jane Grey
40. The Italian scientist Galileo Galilei was known for work in the fields of philosophy, physics, mathematics, and perhaps most famously…
    a. Biology
    b. Geology
    c. Astronomy
    d. Agronomy
41. This mathematician and astronomer published the *Epitome Astronomiae* in 1621, sealing the heliocentric theory of the solar system as systematically proven and accurate.
    a. John Dee
    b. Johannes Kepler
    c. Geoffrey Chaucer
    d. William Tell
42. William Byrd, the English Renaissance composer, wrote widely for voice and instruments, but especially the organ and this harpsichord forerunner.
    a. Harmonica
    b. Harmonium
    c. Virginal
    d. Piano
43. This Italian word refers to the artistic method of portraying depth in a painting through light and shadow.
    a. Chiaroscuro
    b. Contrapposto
    c. Perspective
    d. Impasto
44. This French mathematician and thinker is often considered the first modern philosopher. He's famous for applying mathematical methods to reasoning and for the quote: *Je pense, donc je suis* or "I think, therefore I am."
    a. Heidigger
    b. Nietzche
    c. Pythagorus
    d. Descartes
45. This Renaissance nun wrote extensively on Christian meditation and prayer even as she initiated an ascetic reform of her own Carmelite order until she died in 1582.
    a. Joan of Arc
    b. Catherine of Aragon
    c. Teresa of Avila
    d. Agnes of Poitiers

Answers

38. **D. Michelangelo.** The city of Florence commissioned a statue of David, an important symbol for Florence, from the 26-year-old Michelangelo for placement in the Cathedral. When the signoria saw the magnificent finished product, they decided it should be in the Piazza, the center of Florentine life, instead. A replica is there today, while the original can be seen in the Accademia Gallery (Accademia, 2019).
39. **A. Elizabeth I.** Though she regularly entertained potential suitors for her hand and kingdom in London, Elizabeth ruled and expanded the British Empire on her own from 1558–1603. She considered herself married to England (Morrill & Greenblatt, 2018).
40. **C. Astronomy.** Galileo's design of a new telescope led him to his early astronomical discoveries, like some of the moons of Jupiter. Later in life, he was put on trial for supporting Coperincus's heliocentric model of the solar system, convicted, and put on house arrest (History.com Editors, 2010e).
41. **B. Johannes Kepler.** Among his many other accomplishments, Kepler was in fact the first to explain planetary motion in our solar system in an accurate way. He is, therefore, the founder of our celestial mechanics (Gould, 2017).
42. **C. Virginal.** Though a string keyboard instrument like the harpsichord or piano, in a virginal, the string is plucked rather than being struck. (Editors of Encyclopaedia Britannica, 1998b).
43. **A. Chiaroscuro.** Caravaggio is considered one of the masters of chiaroscuro in painting, and before him it was Titian, the great Venetian painter. This method of adding depth to a 2d surface by painting light was revolutionary—and has an incredible emotional impact even on modern viewers.
44. **D. Descartes.** He developed a theory of dualism between two dimensions of human existence: the mind, which is in essence thought, and the body or matter, which exists in a space of three dimensions (Watson, 2019).
45. **C. Teresa of Avila.** She was canonized in 1622, and her writings are to this day considered the classical example of the ascetic, contemplative life (Editors of Encyclopedia Britannica, 2018b).

Questions

46. This future ruler of Wallachia was held hostage by the Ottoman Empire, along with his younger brother Radu, and then had to fight for almost a decade to regain his father's kingdom.
    a. Vlad III
    b. Wenceslaus IV
    c. Boleslaw the Brave
    d. Maximillian III
47. While hand-held gunpowder projectile weapons existed in China and even Europe previously, the first real, full-powered gunpowder explosive weapons were these massive guns that transformed siege warfare.
    a. Parapets
    b. Cannons
    c. Pistols
    d. Muskets
48. This milestone of sanitary technology was first introduced by Queen Elizabeth I of England's godson in 1596.
    a. Aqueducts
    b. Public baths
    c. Flushing toilet
    d. Drainpipes
49. The Dutch father-and-son team of Hans and Zacharias Janssen created this clutch item for modern scientific exploration by combining more than one curved lens.
    a. Microscope
    b. Television
    c. Spectacles
    d. Window panes
50. This late Renaissance Italian painter, celebrated in her time but neglected by scholars almost up to the modern era, created unforgettably dynamic, fresh scenes of subjects like *Lucretia* and *Susanna and the Elders*.
    a. Mary Cassat
    b. Artemisia Gentileschi
    c. Judith Leyster
    d. Lee Krasner

Answers

46. **A. Vlad III.** The son of Vlad Dracul, aka Dracula and Vlad the Impaler, Vlad III is most infamous for his occasional habit of using impaled enemies on giant spikes to terrorize invading armies. And there was almost always an invading army, during his rule (Wilde, 2019).
47. **B. Cannons.** Wrought-iron cannons, far less likely to explode and kill their operators before the enemy was even within range, were called bombards or lombards (Guilmartin, 2023).
48. **C. Flushing Toilet.** Sir John Harrington was, perhaps, not the greatest poet at the Elizabethan court. He was, however, the inventor of the first flushing toilet. It didn't quite take off with the nobles until much later, but he still gets the credit (Lienhard, n.d.-a).
49. **A. Microscope.** The idea behind it was to have one lens pick up the image and another to magnify it. Astronomers like Galileo and Kepler picked up on this for telescopes almost immediately (theCollector, 2022).
50. **B. Artemisia Gentileschi.** She was raised in the Roman workshop of her father, Orazio, also a painter, but surpassed him quickly in skill according to his own letters. She's also notable for being a woman who fought back against sexual assault at a time when most women ddin't feel safe doing so—her father backed her up in court, and she won (Gasparotto, 2021).

Chapter 6:

Shiny Things: The Golden Age of Exploration

The European Age of Exploration or the Age of Discovery overlaps somewhat with the Renaissance—and certainly fueled many of its changes—but it's also its own phenomenon and extended for some time after the Renaissance had petered out otherwise.

It was a hungry time in Europe, where rich Europeans sponsored intrepid sailors and captains to seek out the "new world" (which was quite old to its present inhabitants) and bring back any resources it yielded. These resources could be produce, ores and metals (in particular, gold), or even human beings.

Massive scientific leaps were made in Europe thanks to the relentless exploration of this period. New species of plant and animal, new metals, new cultures—European explorers encountered all manner of new-to-them things, people, and situations during this age. A method of quantifying things, of comparing and contrasting things, followed. We still use the methods developed in this period in laboratories in the 21st century.

You'll find some timeline overlap with "Chapter 4: Ancient American Splendor: Maya, Inca, and Aztec Empires" in this chapter. Questions that involve indigenous Americans within those larger groups will be in that chapter, and the many, many other indigenous Americans, Caribbeans, and Africans who impacted and were impacted by the Age of Discovery will be in this chapter.

Questions

1. Although these years of European expansion are often referred to as "The Age of Discovery" or "The Age of Exploration," indigenous people already occupied almost all of the lands supposedly discovered or explored during these years.
    a. 100 B.C.–300
    b. 200–1000
    c. 1400–1700
    d. 1500–2000
2. This early Italian explorer who spent time at Kublai Khan's court in the late 13th century wrote a book about his travels that inspired many later explorers.
    a. Amerigo Vespucci
    b. Marco Polo
    c. Vasco de Gama
    d. Francis Drake
3. The Age of Exploration brought so much new information about plants, animals, and the natural world, plus major advances in sailing and cartography. All of this, plus the Renaissance, contributed to this major thought revolution.
    a. The French Revolution
    b. The American Revolution
    c. The Scientific Revolution
    d. The Industrial Revolution
4. The Age of Discovery is generally reckoned to begin in 1434, when Portuguese captain Gil Eanes first sailed around this West African Cape, previously avoided by European sailors.
    a. The Cape of Good Hope
    b. Cape Bojador
    c. Cape Fear
    d. Cape Cod
5. As far as we know, this island off the Iberian peninsula was uninhabited when it was discovered by Portuguese sailors in 1418.
    a. Madeira
    b. Ibiza
    c. Grand Cayman
    d. Bali
6. This Portuguese nobleman sponsored so many ocean voyages that he acquired a maritime nickname.
    a. Captain Kidd
    b. Davy Jones
    c. Baron Galley
    d. Prince Henry the Navigator
7. The oldest records of African people being abducted by Europeans for the purposes of slavery are from…
    a. 1441
    b. 1619
    c. 1602
    d. 1502
8. This navigational tool was invented in China around the year 200, but was commonly used by European sailors by the 15th century.
    a. Sextant
    b. Magnetic compass
    c. Watch
    d. Astrolabe

Answers

1. **C. 1400–1700.** Though these lands were already inhabited, the world did become figuratively "smaller," as in more connected, and peoples more farflung during these centuries of initial European exploration (Briney, 2020).
2. **B. Marco Polo.** His travels on the Silk Road trade routes on behalf of his Venetian merchant family may have been slightly exaggerated, but continue to fascinate and awe to this day (History.com Editors, 2018aa).
3. **C. The Scientific Revolution.** Although the Renaissance was looking back to the classical era for inspiration, the Scientific Revolution taught humanity to think about the natural world quite differently from how the Greeks and Romans did. The scientific method, based on reasoning and observation, still rules to this day (Brain, 2020).
4. **B. Cape Bojador.** This headland off Western Sahara is surrounded by treacherous reefs that gave it the nickname, "The Point of No Return" for European sailors previous to Eanes's attempt had a superstitious fear of it (Editors of Encyclopaedia Britannica, 2021a).
5. **A. Madeira.** João Gonçalves Zarco and Tristão Vaz Teixeira found the heavily-wooded island when a storm drove them off course. They returned with Bartolomeu Perestrello to claim it for Portugal soon after (Davide, 2019).
6. **D. Prince Henry the Navigator.** In spite of never making an exploratory ocean trip himself, Prince Henry sponsored many exploratory voyages in search of other Christian people, a sea route to the east, and—most importantly—gold (PBS, n.d.).
7. **A. 1441.** In modern-day Mauritania, Portuguese sailors captured 12 men and took them back to Portugal as slaves. It's possible the Atlantic slave trade began earlier, however (Ponti, 2019).
8. **B. Magnetic compass.** By the 15th century, navigators had also noticed that the magnetized needle pointed not to the Earth's north pole, but to the magnetic north. Nearer to the equator, this doesn't matter, but nearer the poles, it has to be corrected for (National Geographic Society, 2022l).

Questions

9. Where trade routes had once been mostly coastal, the Age of Exploration saw them branch out into the open seas, bringing different nations into conflict over ocean sovereignty and the concept of *mare liberum* or "open sea" and…
    a. *Pax romana*
    b. *Mare Atlantic*
    c. *Vox populi*
    d. *Mare Clausum*
10. Continuing the tradition of Portuguese trailblazers, this man's fleet was the first European one to round the southern tip of Africa, the Cape of Good Hope.
    a. Bartolomeu Dias
    b. Christopher Colombus
    c. Hernán Cortés
    d. Francisco Pizarro
11. While the search for better trade routes, new resources, and gold were all major motivations for European exploration, this motive was even more imperative for some.
    a. The spread of Christianity
    b. Making friends
    c. The spread of art and music
    d. Holidays
12. European monarchs didn't sponsor exploration for the sake of curiosity, but for the sake of…
    a. Fun
    b. Cultural exchange
    c. Commerce
    d. Feeding the poor
13. This Portuguese captain was the first to reach India by sea, but his dealings with the Zamorin or king of Calicut (in modern-day Kerala) were a failure.
    a. Pedro Álvares Cabral
    b. Magellan
    c. James Cook
    d. Vasco da Gama
14. This treaty between Spain and Portugal divided up the "New World" between them—utterly disregarding the extant nations already occupying the Americas.
    a. Treaty of Tordesillas
    b. Treaty of Versailles
    c. Treaty of Paris
    d. Treaty of Andalusia
15. This explorer was attempting to find a sea route to India for the King and Queen of Spain when he stumbled across the Carribean islands in 1492.
    a. Toby Sanchez
    b. Christopher Columbus
    c. Vasco da Gama
    d. Simon Bolivar
16. After Columbus's voyages to the Americas, the exchange of crops, animals, microbes, and other biological components between the New and Old World is referred to as…
    a. The Galapagos Effect
    b. The Haitian Exchange
    c. The Brazilian Connection
    d. The Columbian Exchange

Answers

9. **D. *Mare Clausum.*** Latin for "closed sea," this legal term indicates a sea that is closed to traffic for any but its sovereign nation. Spain and Portugal in particular grasped many of these rights in the early years of the Age—France, The Netherlands, and England tended to ignore it (Theutenberg, 1984).
10. **A. Bartolomeu Dias.** In the 1450s, the overland trade routes to the east were shut down to Europeans when the Ottoman Empire acquired the last of the Byzantine Empire's holdings. They needed a sea route, and he found it (History.com Editors, 2018f).
11. **A. The Spread of Christianity.** As soon as the Catholic Church in Rome heard about "new" indigenous peoples in Africa, Australia, and the Americas, they sent wave after wave of clergy to convert—sometimes peacefully, often forcibly, if necessary.
12. **C. Commerce.** Explorers were sent out from the great courts of Europe to enrich those courts with resources, particularly gold and slaves. So while individual captains and sailors may have had a spirit of adventure, it was also a business transaction on a larger scale.
13. **D. Vasco da Gama.** He returned with 20 ships years later at the behest of Manuel I of Portugal, in order to demand tribute. At the Battle of Calicut in 1503, da Gama's fleet crushed the Zamorin's forces… but still failed to extract tribute (Beyer, 2023a).
14. **A. Treaty of Tordesillas.** This treaty is why, to this day, while half of South America speaks Spanish, Brazil speaks Portuguese, and indigenous languages were repressed for so long (National Geographic Society, 2022j).
15. **B. Christopher Columbus.** He searched for gold throughout the islands, with the help of enslaved locals, and set up a settlement on Hispaniola. He and his brothers managed to decimate the indigenous Taino population within 60 years of mismanagement (History.com Editors, 2009k).
16. **D. The Columbian Exchange.** The Continental Drift that pulled the Americas apart from the rest of the world had allowed life to evolve separately on both sides of the world since then. Now animals, plants, and diseases flowed between both hemispheres of the globe (McNeill, 2022).

Questions

17. This simple tool invented by Arabian sailors in the 9th century helped sailors in the Age of Exploration to navigate the stars via the mathematical relations within triangles.
    a. The kamal
    b. The stopwatch
    c. The dove
    d. The compass
18. The Portuguese had the latest in sailing technology, including these deep, broad, oceangoing ships with 3 (sometimes 4) masts.
    a. Landsharks
    b. Carracks
    c. Bayliners
    d. Bonaventures
19. These large ships were developed in the 16th century from less-protected merchant vessels, mainly for war, as in the Spanish Armada, and protection of imported colonial goods.
    a. Galleons
    b. Canoes
    c. Battleships
    d. Bayliners
20. These maps and charts were mainly drawn on vellum, and served the purpose of helping sailors find ports and harbors.
    a. Relief
    b. Political
    c. Elevation
    d. Portolan
21. Slave traders from Europe took a three-part journey: the first being from Europe to Africa's West Coast, where they'd load hundreds of people into cramped cargo holds, and then this, the most dangerous leg of the journey.
    a. The Middle Passage
    b. The Trail of Tears
    c. The Seasickness
    d. The Plank
22. This type of slavery fed the need for labor in new colonies during the European Age of Exploration, not to be confused with bonded or forced labor slavery.
    a. Child labor
    b. Trafficking
    c. Indentured
    d. Chattel
23. The marriage of Ferdinand II of Aragon and this queen unified a divided Spain once and for all.
    a. Eleanor of Aquitaine
    b. Joan of Castile
    c. Joanna the Mad
    d. Isabella I of Castile
24. Jorge Álvares was the first European explorer to reach this country by sea.
    a. India
    b. Thailand
    c. China
    d. Canada

Answers

17. **A. The kamal.** This simple-looking tool, made of a flat piece of wood and a string, for the most part, helped sailors discover their latitude by measuring the elevation of stars (Nielbock, 2018).
18. **B. Carracks.** Portuguese and Spanish ship-builders developed the carrack by taking the best qualities of Mediterranean and North Atlantic types of ships for trade. It became the favorite ship of explorers of this age (Editors of Encyclopaedia Britannica, 2021b).
19. **A. Galleons.** These ships were built with two rows of cannon on each side and an elongated hull shape for stability. They also made good merchant vessels in time of peace, though they were smaller than most Carracks.
20. **D. Portolan.** Considered to be the very first professional cartography in the world, Portolan charts have rhumb lines radiating out from their center to help navigators plot courses and find safe harbor. Although the Vikings had navigated across the Atlantic long before the Age of Discovery, their techniques had been lost by that time. Sailing along a coast was the only sure bet (Editors of Encyclopaedia Britannica, 1998a).
21. **A. The Middle Passage.** So called because it was the second leg of the journey; the third was the return to Europe from the Americas. The Middle Passage was notoriously perilous, with Africans aboard subjected to cramped conditions, disease, malnourishment, and abuse from their captors (PBS, 2019).
22. **D. Chattel.** In chattel slavery, the slave is legally reduced to a tool or object, the property of their owner in perpetuity. They could be bought, sold, or used as their owner saw fit for either domestic or production duties. In some societies, there were legal limits placed on such things, but any protections for slaves were exceedingly rare during the Transatlantic Slave Trade (Asante, 2007).
23. **D. Isabella I of Castile.** This Spanish power couple not only united Spain, laying the groundwork for its modern incarnation, but also took it upon themselves to spread Catholicism all over their own domain and to the New World. They got very rich doing it (Lockett, 2022).
24. **C. China.** Álvares is even said to have founded a Euro-Chinese settlement called Tamão somewhere between Macau (where he first landed) and modern Hong Kong, though scholars can't agree where it was exactly (O'Connell, 2021).

Questions

25. The Ribeira das Naus in this European city served as the major shipbuilding hub for both the formal and informal Portuguese empires.
    a. Cannes
    b. Lisbon
    c. Gibraltar
    d. Stockholm
26. The Age of Exploration is woven deeply into the fabric of Portuguese culture, as proven by Luís de Camões's seminal epic poem, *Os Lusíadas*, about this explorer's journey to India.
    a. Hernán Cortés
    b. Álvar Núñez Cabeza de Vaca
    c. Vasco da Gama
    d. William Perry
27. Juan Ponce de León, a Spanish explorer and governor of Puerto Rico, followed rumors of this mythical object all the way to modern-day Florida.
    a. Atlantis
    b. The Fountain of Youth
    c. The Golden City
    d. The Keys
28. This Venetian navigator sailed under the English flag with an English name—and laid the groundwork for England's claim on Canada by finding Newfoundland.
    a. John Cabot
    b. Richard Harris
    c. Francis Drake
    d. Prince Henry the Navigator
29. Elizabeth I of England, the last Tudor monarch, sponsored many excursions to the New World for the purposes of colonization and capital. Most famously, she funded Sir Frances Drake and this court favorite.
    a. Christopher Columbus
    b. Walter Raleigh
    c. Francis Walsingham
    d. James Stuart
30. Martin Waldseemüller took on the ambitious project of creating a new world map in 1507. He named the Americas for this Italian explorer, who'd recognized during his 1501–1502 voyage that this was a new continent.
    a. Amerigo Vespucci
    b. Christopher Columbus
    c. Ferdinand Magellan
    d. Leif Eriksson
31. This American cash crop was introduced all over Europe in the 1550s and 60s, though European settlers didn't manage to grow it for themselves until John Rolfe in 1612.
    a. Hay
    b. Lima beans
    c. Quinoa
    d. Tobacco
32. This Portuguese explorer, sailing under the flag of Spain, was the first European to cross the Pacific Ocean and circle the globe by sea—even if he died in the process.
    a. Ferdinand Magellan
    b. Charles Darwin
    c. Ponce de León
    d. Antonio de Abreu

Answers

25. **B. Lisbon.** Brazil, with its high-quality forests, often exported wood to Lisbon, where it'd be made into ships at Ribeira das Naus. There were shipbuilding outposts in the Pacific, too, such as in India (Polónia & Oliveira, 2019).
26. **C. Vasco da Gama.** *Os Lusíadas* (1572) drops hints that Camões might've been to India himself in service of the king, but little is known about his life. His poetry, on the other hand, is unparalleled in importance in Portuguese literature (Editors of Encyclopedia Britannica, 2023).
27. **B. The Fountain of Youth.** Ponce de León was looking for an island called Bimini where, according to indigenous peoples, there was a magical spring that would heal and rejuvenate anyone who drank from it (History.com Editors, 2018k).
28. **A. John Cabot.** Giovanni Caboto also had the idea to sail west and find Asia, completely separate from his slightly more famous contemporary fellow-Italian, Christopher Columbus (JCU, 2019).
29. **B. Walter Raleigh.** Sir Walter has often been said to have charmed Queen Elizabeth into funding his excursions and attempts at colonies on the eastern seaboard of the modern-day United States.
30. **A. Amerigo Vespucci.** Though Vespucci only visited South America, later mapmakers simply put his name on both Northern and Southern landmasses, thus handing him most of the European credit (Biography.com, 2021).
31. **D. Tobacco.** Mostly smoked in pipes for ceremonial or medicinal purposes among indigenous people, tobacco became popular for recreation overseas very quickly after it was introduced (CNN, 2019).
32. **A. Magellan.** Ferdinand Magellan or Fernão de Magalhães renounced his Portuguese citizenship after King Manuel repeatedly refused his proposal to sail to the Spice Islands. King Charles I of Spain was far more interested (History.com Editors, 2018ac).

Questions

33. This Spanish conquistador sailed with Balboa when he "discovered" the Pacific Ocean and later led the bloody Spanish charge into Inca territory in modern-day Peru.
    a. Francis Drake
    b. Francisco Pizzaro
    c. Pedro Arias Dávila
    d. Pedro de los Ríos
34. The Conquistador Hernando de Soto fought in Peru before becoming the first European to cross this great North American River.
    a. Colorado
    b. Rio Grande
    c. Mississippi
    d. Delaware
35. In 1553, Sir Hugh Willoughby tried to navigate to Asia by way of this route that runs largely along the north coast of Siberia.
    a. The Strait of Magellan
    b. The Panama Canal
    c. The Bering Sea
    d. The Northeast Passage
36. Sir Francis Drake was famous as a mariner and naval captain in his own time, but also in his capacity as this kind of state-sanctioned pirate.
    a. Tax collector
    b. Privateer
    c. Boatswain
    d. Pilot
37. This English Captain, who sailed all over the Eastern seaboard of the United States, was ultimately killed in a mutiny in the Bay that bears his name today.
    a. Henry Hudson
    b. Delaware McCoy
    c. William Baffin
    d. Francisco Pizarro
38. Étienne Brûlé explored the modern-day Great Lakes area in the early 1600s in Canada–which was called this, at that time.
    a. New France
    b. New Foundland
    c. Greenland
    d. Iceland
39. The French explorer Jean Nicollet acted as diplomat to multiple First Nations people in modern-day Canada, including the Huron and…
    a. Cherokee
    b. Winnebago
    c. Hopi
    d. Inupiaq
40. La Malinche was the daughter of an Aztec *cacique* who was sold into slavery, then worked as a guide/interpreter for this conquistador.
    a. Vasco da Gama
    b. Hernando Cortés
    c. Francisco Pizarro
    d. Hernando de Soto

Answers

33. **B. Francisco Pizarro.** Pizarro was ultimately assassinated by agents of his former ally, Diego de Almagro, who took over Cuzco for himself. But not before he caused a great deal of damage to Inca people and civilization (History.com Editors, 2018x).
34. **C. Mississippi.** De Soto died of a fever on May 21, 1542, and his men buried him in the Mississippi river before taking rafts back down to Mexico (History.com Editors, 2018j).
35. **D. The Northeast Passage.** In 1554, Willoughby and two of his three ships were found at anchor in Lapland, dead to a man. Only the men on the first ship survived, and they were separated from the other two in a storm (Gordon, 1986).
36. **B. Privateer.** During their war with Spain, Drake was commissioned by Queen Elizabeth to plunder Spanish ports in the New World. He also sailed around the world via the straits of Magellan under the English flag (History.com Editors, 2009p).
37. **A. Henry Hudson.** He also sailed up the modern-day Hudson River, thinking it might be a canal that would open into the Pacific Ocean. It was not (History.com Editors, 2018z).
38. **A. New France.** Brûlé emigrated to modern-day Ontario in 1608 and lived out the rest of his life there, exploring its land and people (Editors of Encyclopaedia Britannica, 2023c).
39. **B. Winnebago.** This nation called themselves the "People of the Sea," and Nicollet was one of the first Europeans to encounter and become an ambassador to them (Canadian Museum of History, n.d.).
40. **B. Hernando Cortés.** Although it's often said that La Malinche became Cortés's mistress, there's no real evidence of that—only that she was an indigenous woman sold as a slave, who saved his life more than once with her keen powers of observation and translation (Mohammed, 2019).

Questions

41. French explorer Robert de La Salle is often credited as being the first European to see this large North American River, for which we still use the Iroquois name.
    a. New River
    b. Yellowstone River
    c. Yukon River
    d. Ohio River
42. This Russian Emperor commissioned the first Kamchatka Expedition in 1725, with an eye to discovering whether North America and Russia were really divided by an ocean or not.
    a. Catherine the Great
    b. Peter the Great
    c. Ivan the Terrible
    d. Nicholas I
43. This island in the South-Pacific is famous for its Moai, large, stylized statues, many of which were built by the indigenous Polynesian people centuries before Europeans first saw them in 1722.
    a. Tasmania
    b. Singapore
    c. Easter Island
    d. Maui
44. Alaska was first explored by Russian Naval officers Chirikov and his leader, a Danish explorer after whom the strait between Alaska and Russia is named.
    a. Søren Kierkegaard
    b. Leif Eriksson
    c. Axel Berg
    d. Vitus Bering
45. Captain James Cook's crew were the first Europeans to interact with the indigenous people of these Pacific islands.
    a. Singapore
    b. Fiji
    c. Hawaii
    d. Sri Lanka
46. Though the first European to catch sight of this Pacific Island, Abel Tasman, tried to name it for his patron Van Diemen's Land, his own name stuck instead.
    a. Tasmania
    b. Australia
    c. Bali
    d. Abelswith
47. These two staple crops, now integral to diets all over the world, were only found in the Americas before the 1500s.
    a. Rice and wheat
    b. Soybeans and barley
    c. Corn and potatoes
    d. Wheat and corn

Answers

41. **D. Ohio River.** Robert Cavelier, Sieur de LaSalle, took up his North American explorations on behalf of Louis XIV of France. In 1669, he came to the Ohio River thanks to his indigenous guides. Sadly, the river did not take him to China or Japan as he'd hoped (KY Historical Society, n.d.).
42. **B. Peter the Great.** Not long before his death, Peter the Great ordered the first Kamchatka Expedition. The second one was made to explore modern-day Alaska (Library of Congress, n.d.).
43. **C. Easter Island.** So-called by Dutch explorer Jacob Roggeveen because he first spotted it on Easter Sunday, 1722, the indigenous people who still call it home know it as Rapa Nui (Trachtman, 2002).
44. **D. Bering.** Though he was Danish, Vitus Bering spent most of his life in Peter the Great's navy (Lewis, 2019b).
45. **C. Hawaii.** While at first Cook's crew was able to exploit the indigenous Hawaiians' curiosity about their ships, attire, and even weapons, eventually relations turned sour. Cook was ultimately killed by the people he and his crew had tried to exploit (History.com Editors, 2019i).
46. **A. Tasmania.** Like Australia, Tasmania was used as a place to "transport" criminals who were banished from their home countries like England in Europe—in spite of the indigenous people who'd been living there for centuries before them (Newman, 2006).
47. **C. Corn and potatoes.** At first, many Europeans wouldn't eat potatoes and even thought they might be poisonous. They were more often fed to livestock than humans in the old world for decades after they were discovered in Peru (Potatoes USA, n.d.).

Questions

48. Tomatoes were first domesticated in this modern-day country—and despite their popularity in many cuisines today, didn't gain popularity in Europe until the 19th century.
    a. The United States
    b. Mexico
    c. Brazil
    d. Ecuador
49. European attitudes toward existing indigenous peoples were reinforced by this Papal law from 1493.
    a. Magna Carta
    b. Romanus Pontifex
    c. Manifest Destiny
    d. Doctrine of Discovery
50. This was the first woman to circumnavigate the globe, which she did on Louis Antoine de Bougainville's *Etoile* from 1776–1779.
    a. Jeanne Baret
    b. Amelia Earhart
    c. Mary Wollstonecraft
    d. Mary Shelley

Answers

48. **B. Mexico.** It's hard to think of Italian food without tomatoes, today, but for a long time tomatoes were suspect by Europeans, since they're related to deadly nightshade (Roos, 2021b).
49. **D. Doctrine of Discovery.** The 1493 Papal Bull called *Inter Caetera* made it clear that, as far as the Pope was concerned, any land not already inhabited by Christians was up for grabs by any Christian power who could bring it into the fold, so to speak. Pope Francis finally renounced this in 2023 (The Gilder Lehrman Institute of American History, n.d.).
50. **A. Jeanne Baret.** Women weren't allowed aboard French Royal Navy ships, but she and her lover, who was a botanist on the voyage, Philibert Commerson, managed to keep her a secret for a while (NPR, 2020).

Chapter 7:

The Great Experiment: The United States of America

George Washington once said of the brand new United States that, "The establishment of our new Government seemed to be the last great experiment for promoting human happiness." (Morgan Library and Museum, 2013). While some might argue that Washington couldn't have known what the fledgling country would experience in the next hundred years, posterity tells us otherwise. Washington—indeed all the founding fathers, mothers, and others of America—knew the contradictions inherent in the very existence of this new nation.

For one, it was built on land that had originally been occupied by many and varied indigenous nations—who now had no voice in the government. For another, the institution of chattel slavery of both stolen African and indigenous American people was directly counter to the belief in "life, liberty, and the pursuit of happiness" declared in the country's founding document, the *Declaration of Independence*. Not to mention that a government "of the people, by the people, and for the people" (a phrase uttered half a century later by President Abraham Lincoln, but still relevant to American-style Democracy even in the early days) had never before been attempted in quite the same way on such a large scale.

For all this fraught inception, the United States' ethos of free speech and free minds quickly made it a forerunner in economics and world politics. Inventors, artists, philosophers, and businesspeople abounded almost from the start. A nation of contradictions, of proudly protected personal freedoms, and of loud opinions, the American Experiment is still going strong to this day.

Questions

1. This city was the first permanent European settlement in the modern-day United States of America.
    a. St. Augustine, Florida
    b. Plymouth, Massachusetts
    c. Charlotte, North Carolina
    d. New Orleans, Louisiana
2. When French Huguenots settled near the first Spanish settlement in Florida, this outraged Spanish king sent troops to clear them out and replace them.
    a. Charles V
    b. Phillip II
    c. Francis I
    d. Manuel I
3. The first indigenous people to deal with English settlers in Virginia were this confederacy of Algonquian-speaking tribes and villages.
    a. Hopi
    b. Mexica
    c. Cherokee
    d. Powhatan
4. This captain and Jamestown leader wrote a seminal first-hand account of the colony called *The Generall Historie of Virginia* in 1624
    a. John Smith
    b. Christopher Columbus
    c. Thomas Jefferson
    d. Virginia Dare
5. These indigenous people were the first to deal with Pilgrims attempting to start a new colony at Plymouth, Massachusetts.
    a. Navajo
    b. Inuit
    c. Pokanoket Wampanoag
    d. Mohawk Iroquois
6. The first ship carrying Africans to be sold as slaves in the Virginia colony landed in this year, marking the beginning of race-based chattel slavery in the United States.
    a. 1590
    b. 1810
    c. 1619
    d. 1700
7. While over 500 different tribes or nations lived in California before the 1500s, the first white settlers were mainly Spanish…
    a. Fishermen
    b. Missionaries
    c. Architects
    d. Soldiers
8. Many indigenous nations lived in modern-day Louisiana 10,000 years or more before the French settled there, including the…
    a. Navajo and Hopi
    b. Natchez and Tunica
    c. Seminole and Cherokee
    d. Apache and Arapaho

Answers

1. **A. St. Augustine, Florida.** Settled by a Spanish soldier called Pedro Menéndez de Avilés in 1565, the settlement was named for the day it was founded, August 28, the feast of St. Augustine. Centuries before he arrived, the Timucua people had settled there (Kiger, 2020).
2. **B. Phillip II.** Considering both that the French had no business in his new colony *and* that Protestants like the Huguenots should be wiped out, the Catholic hardliner Phillip sent his troops to do just that. The Hugeuenots were massacred (Bryant, 2020).
3. **D. Powhatan.** Powhatan united the scattered Algonquian tribes of Virginia and Delaware in the late 1500s. They spent a century alternately helping, being attacked by, and attacking Jamestown settlers in their territory (Kosa & Johnson, 2018).
4. **A. John Smith.** The book's full title is: *The Generall Historie of Virginia, New-England, and the Summer Isles: With the Names of the Adventurers, Planters, and Governours from Their First Beginning, Ano: 1584. To This Present 1624. With the Procedings of Those Severall Colonies and the Accidents That Befell Them in All Their Journyes and Discoveries. Also the Maps and Descriptions of All Those Countryes, Their Commodities, People, Government, Customes, and Religion Yet Knowne. Divided into Sixe Bookes. By Captaine Iohn Smith, Sometymes Governour in Those Countryes & Admirall of New England.*
5. **C. Pokanoket Wampanoag.** The Pokanoket leader, Massasoit, treated with the Pilgrim's who'd come over on the Mayflower via a Pawtuxet interpreter, Tisquantum or Squanto, who'd been kidnapped and taken to England years earlier (History.com Editors, 2019j).
6. **C. 1619.** The African laborers aboard the *White Lion* were traded for supplies. Originally captured by the Spanish slave ship *San Juan Bautista*, they'd then been recaptured by English privateers and brought to Virginia. This was just the beginning of America's long and fraught history with the trans-Atlantic slave trade (Cochran, n.d.).
7. **B. Missionaries.** Spanish missionaries served the dual purpose of saving indigenous souls and indoctrinating the local Californians about how to be good Spanish citizens. In 1821, when Mexico won its independence, California passed to Mexico. Then in 1847, during the Mexican-American war, California was surrendered to the United States (History.com Editors, 2009h).
8. **B. Natchez and Tunica.** These nations had their own wars with each other, which the French and British only complicated when they arrived. The Tunica allied with the French against the British. The Natchez fought the Choctaw allied with the French (History.com Editors, 2019k).

Questions

9. Although North American colonies were more a drain than a source of resources at first, by 1770 they were an important source of many exports for the French and British, including…
   a. Tobacco and furs
   b. Pepper and salt
   c. Cinnamon and nutmeg
   d. Silk and Satin
10. This final English colony in modern-day America was founded by James Oglethorpe, who insisted it distribute land fairly to those who needed it and prohibited slavery at the outset.
    a. South Carolina
    b. Florida
    c. Delaware
    d. Georgia
11. This conflict, better known in America as the French and Indian War, dragged on from 1756–1763; Spain, England, and France battled for colonies in the Americas and Prussia battled Austria, France, Russia and Sweden in Europe.
    a. Crimean War
    b. Hundred Years' War
    c. Tripolitan War
    d. Seven Years' War
12. Colonists in Boston protested a series of royal acts that increased taxation on certain imports with this event in Boston Harbor on December 16, 1773.
    a. The Boston Tea Party
    b. Occupy Wall Street
    c. The Stonewall Riot
    d. The Greensboro Sit-in
13. These battles, fought on April 19, 1775, are considered the official kickoff to the American Revolution.
    a. York and Edinburgh
    b. New York and Boston
    c. Lexington and Concord
    d. Salem and Winston
14. Of the six nations that comprised the Iroquois Confederacy in modern-day New York, only this many supported the Americans in their revolution; the rest sided with the English.
    a. 4
    b. 5
    c. 1
    d. 2
15. Lord Dunmore's Proclamation of 1775 aimed to weaken American revolutionary power in Virginia by declaring martial law and…
    a. Declaring that he was the King of Virginia
    b. Offering freedom to any slave who'd fight for the British
    c. Giving all British soldiers free land in Virginia
    d. Offering a case of rum to all British conscripts

Answers

9. **A. Tobacco and furs.** By the 1770s, the lean days of these colonies were mostly behind them—well-off white colonists had a comparable lifestyle to their Continental counterparts. (National Museum of American History 2018).
10. **D. Georgia.** Named for the current English sovereign, George III, the colony started out as intended, but the colonists soon rebelled against all the restrictions put upon them when compared to neighboring colonies. Larger plots of land and slavery were all allowed by the 1740s (Library of Congress, n.d.).
11. **D. Seven Years' War.** The end of this conflict was signaled by the The Treaty of Paris for the American theater and the Treaty of Hubertusburg for the European theater (History.com Editors, 2009m).
12. **A. The Boston Tea Party.** The Sugar Act and Stamp Act, the Townshend Duties, and finally the Tea Act were all import and export duties imposed upon the American colonies—who had no representation in Parliament—by England. The Sons of Liberty protested by dumping 342 chests of East India Company tea into the harbor (History.com Editors, 2009c).
13. **C. Lexington and Concord.** Paul Revere's famous midnight ride was conducted the night before to warn of British Troops mobilizing out of Boston—but far from shouting his warning, he was as covert as possible to avoid being caught by the British Army (History.com Editors, 2018ab).
14. **D. 2.** The Oneida and Tuscarora sided with the Americans. The Mohawk, Onondaga, Cayuga, and Seneca understandably decided that they'd have better luck dealing with the British, who at least put some strictures on their white settlers (Makos, 2021).
15. **B. Offering freedom to any slave who'd fight for the British.** Although the institution of African chattel slavery was tacitly endorsed by the British government, who allowed the slave trade to flourish for their enrichment, they knew Southern money and power was dependant on slave labor (Gilder Lehrman Institute of American History, n.d.).

Questions

16. America's Commander-in-Chief Washington fought many battles during the Revolutionary war, but only definitively won five, including this one that ended in British surrender.
    a. Yorktown
    b. Boston
    c. Trenton
    d. Kip's Bay
17. The Treaty of Paris, at the end of the French and Indian War, was so favorable to the British that it was partially responsible for this European power siding with the American revolutionaries.
    a. Spain
    b. Portugal
    c. Hungary
    d. France
18. Many adherents to this pacifist Christian sect joined in the American revolution in their own way, such as the spy Lydia Darragh, or even took up arms in direct conflict with their beliefs.
    a. Amish
    b. Quaker
    c. Presbyterian
    d. Catholic
19. This precursor to the United States Constitution was adopted by every state in the Union by 1781.
    a. Magna Carta
    b. Bill of Rights
    c. Promise Ring
    d. Articles of Confederation
20. The United States purchased this territory from France in 1803 for $11,250,000 and the assumption of some debts.
    a. Oregon
    b. Montana
    c. Louisiana
    d. Maine
21. This invention of Eli Whitney's, while ingenious, increased the demand for labor on southern plantations as cotton became a bigger cash crop.
    a. The cotton gin
    b. The steam engine
    c. The pedal sewing machine
    d. The printing press
22. Versions of this Federal act were passed in 1793 and 1850 to pacify Southern lawmakers.
    a. Volstead Act
    b. Fugitive Slave Act
    c. Civil Rights Act
    d. Homestead Act
23. Westward expansion by European settlers was put in fast-forward by the discovery of this in California in 1848.
    a. Aliens
    b. Ruins
    c. Forests
    d. Gold

Answers

16. **A. Yorktown.** Washington pinned British General Cornwallis down in Yorktown while his French naval allies made sure no British reinforcements could arrive via the Chesapeake Bay. Cornwallis surrendered on October 19, 1781 (Mount Vernon Ladies' Association, 2019).
17. **D. France.** Thanks largely to Benjamin Franklin's ambassadorship in Paris and the Marquis de Lafayette's revolutionary sensibilities, Louis XVI agreed to send ships to help the Americans. That help was definitive.
18. **B. Quaker.** Many Quakers emigrated from Europe to the Americas for the freedom of religion they found there. During the Revolution, many of them were exiled, jailed, and persecuted for refusing to fight (Johnson, 2022).
19. **D. Articles of Confederation.** When these articles proved too weak to provide a unified diplomatic front between the states, the Constitutional Convention was convened (Office of the Historian, 2019).
20. **C. Louisiana.** The Louisiana Purchase was a great deal for President Thomas Jefferson, coming in at about 3 cents per acre. 9 years later, Louisiana became the 18th US state (History. com Editors, 2009).
21. **A. The cotton gin.** Whitney's invention made it easier to separate cotton seeds from the soft cotton fibers, which meant that short-staple cotton, which flourished in a larger geographic area than the coastally friendly long-stable, suddenly became viable (History.com Editors, 2019).
22. **B. The Fugitive Slave Act.** Both of these Acts were legal band-aids to keep America from splitting in half over the issue of slavery: the south thought the north made it impossible to enforce them, and the north, in most cases, simply ignored them. They were finally repealed in 1864, during the Civil War (History.com Editors, 2018y).
23. **D. Gold.** Between 1848 and 1849, the white population of California went from less than 1000 to over 1000 as settlers rushed to the area around San Francisco. This was the beginning of the California Gold Rush and the fascination with America's "wild" west (History.com Editors, 2010a).

Questions

24. Harriet Tubman worked as a "conductor" on this metaphorical transportation system that helped enslaved Americans escape to freedom in Canada.
    a. The Subway
    b. Magellan's Tunnel
    c. The Underground Railroad
    d. The Underwater Boat
25. By the time this 16th President of the United States was inaugurated, seven states had already seceded and the Confederate States of America had formed.
    a. John Quincy Adams
    b. Andrew Jackson
    c. Benjamin Harrison
    d. Abraham Lincoln
26. Modern estimates suggest that between 650,000 and 850,000 Americans died in this war between 1861–1865.
    a. WWI
    b. The Mexican Civil War
    c. The American Civil War
    d. The War of 1812
27. One of the people who developed the Telegraph also developed this eponymous code for spelling out words on it with dashes and dots.
    a. Morse Code
    b. Braille
    c. Semafor
    d. Sign language
28. The Winchester rifle, model 1886, was the first ever to have this, starting off Winchester's reputation as "the gun that won the West."
    a. Break action
    b. Lever-operated repeating action
    c. Left-handed trigger
    d. Silencer
29. The 13th Amendment abolished slavery in the United States. The 14th Amendment defines all people born in the United States as citizens, regardless of race or creed. And the 15th Amendment…
    a. Guarantees every (male) citizen the right to vote, regardless of race or creed.
    b. Guarantees freedom of the press in the United States.
    c. Abolishes loud music after midnight in all urban areas.
    d. Guarantees every American's right to preach their own religion.
30. Most Americans believe this man invented the telephone, but in fact he was only granted the first American patent for it after creating his own version.
    a. Thomas Edison
    b. Nikola Tesla
    c. Albert Einstein
    d. Alexander Graham Bell
31. As a result of this 1830 Act, signed into law by President Andrew Jackson, countless Native Americans, including thousands of Cherokee people, were forced out of their ancestral lands to make way for white settlers east of the Mississippi.
    a. Patriot Act
    b. Indian Removal Act
    c. Civil Rights Act
    d. Winter Act

Answers

24. **C. The Underground Railroad.** This network of abolitionists functioned loosely at first, but gained organization and structure as it became more and more prolific. It was one of the most effective methods of resistance abolitionists had. Although the freed slaves faced prejudice in Canada, at least there, they were free (National Park Service, 2020).
25. **D. Lincoln.** Abraham Lincoln was the first Republican party member to be elected President of the United States. Many southern states had claimed that, if a Republican (as in someone who was against the spread of slavery) was elected, they'd secede from the Union (History.com Editors, 2018e).
26. **C. The American Civil War.** It was a fight that had been simmering since well before the Declaration of Independence in 1776. Half of the country seceded from the Union over a state's right to decide whether or not it allowed slavery within its borders. The Union fought back. (History.com Editors, 2009a).
27. **A. Morse code.** Samuel Morse sent his first telegraph in 1844, and it remained the fastest and most accurate way to communicate around the world until the telephone replaced it in the 20th century (History.com Editors, 2009n).
28. **B. Lever-operated repeating action.** The Winchester repeating rifle was the first reliable gun of its kind in the world, and it gave white settlers in the west a distinct advantage over the indigenous people who'd been living there for millenia (Cuffia, n.d.).
29. **A. Guarantees every (male) citizen the right to vote, regardless of race or creed.** These three are considered the Reconstruction Amendments, passed when the US was trying to rebuild (and check) the south after the devastation of the Civil War (PBS, 2017).
30. **D. Alexander Graham Bell.** Bell's first telephone call, on March 10, 1876, was to his assistant. He said, "Mr Watson, come here—I want to see you." (Science Museum, 2018).
31. **B. Indian Removal Act.** Among tens of thousands of others, about 15000 Cherokee people were forcibly marched west by the army through the fall and winter of 1838–39. Around 4000 of them died on the way, earning their path the name, "The Trail of Tears" (Library of Congress, 2022).

Questions

32. This Shawnee leader allied with the Canandians and English in the war of 1812, hoping to someday achieve his dream of a united Native American Country.
    a. Tecumseh
    b. Tisquantum
    c. Powhatan
    d. Mingo
33. This massive infrastructure project linking the East Coast to the West of the United States started before the Civil War, but didn't finish until after it.
    a. The interstate system
    b. Fiber Optic cable
    c. 5G
    d. The transcontinental railroad
34. Between 1800 and 1890, this large mammal of the Great Plains was hunted to the brink of extinction by white settlers.
    a. Skunk
    b. American bison
    c. Bald eagle
    d. White-tailed deer
35. Sitting Bull and Crazy Horse led this united resistance when the U.S. Gold Rush threatened their sacred Black Hills, granted in a 1868 treaty.
    a. Navajo
    b. Apache
    c. Sioux
    d. Iroquois
36. This railroad and shipping magnate was the richest person in America from 1850 until his death in 1877—and his son and heir was for the next decade.
    a. Jeff Bezos
    b. Cornelius Vanderbilt
    c. Doc Holliday
    d. P.T. Barnum
37. For 60 years, starting in 1892, this island at the mouth of the Hudson River served as the main checkpoint for transatlantic immigration. Now, visitors can see the Museum of Immigration there.
    a. Rhode Island
    b. Alcatraz Island
    c. Ellis Island
    d. Erie Island
38. This transatlantic revolution began with the advent of large factories in Britain in the mid 1800s, but took a few decades to make it to American shores.
    a. The Industrial Revolution
    b. The Velvet Revolution
    c. Revolution 9
    d. The Peoples' Revolution
39. This was the very first of the United States National Parks, signed into being by President Grant in 1872.
    a. Glacier
    b. Redwood
    c. Carlsbad
    d. Yellowstone

Answers

32. **A. Tecumseh.** Tecumseh traveled all over the US making alliances and connections on behalf of his Shawnee nation and his dream of unifying all Native peoples. He saw the British alliance as a way to gain even better footing (National Park Service, 2019).
33. **D. The transcontinental railroad.** On May 10, 1869, the Union Pacific finally hooked up with the Central Pacific at Promontory, Utah. This was the first transcontinental train route in North America (Library of Congress, 2015).
34. **B. American bison.** White settlers didn't just kill bison to eat or use; they wiped out bison by the cartloads to decimate the indigenous plains peoples' economy, much of which was based around the bison. These herds have never recovered completely, although the modern National Parks Service maintains several herds now (Smithsonian's National Zoo, 2018).
35. **C. Sioux.** The Arapaho and Cheyenne joined the Sioux nation to defend their rights during the Great Sioux War. They won the Battle of Little Bighorn—which General Custer had been advised to avoid, but chose not to (National Park Service, 2016).
36. **B. Cornelius Vanderbilt.** This tycoon from Staten Island got his nickname "The Commodore" from owning and operating a huge fleet of steamships. The name Vanderbilt has been a byword for riches in the United States ever since (History.com Editors, 2010b).
37. **C. Ellis Island.** Samuel Ellis purchased the island in 1794, the Dutch owned from then to 1630. Mohegan people lived nearby before that (History.com Editors, 2018h).
38. **A. The Industrial Revolution.** A switch was happening in urban centers around the world, as economies slowly shifted away from purely agricultural and into manufacturing and energy sectors (ushistory.org, 2019).
39. **D. Yellowstone.** The lessons learned by the early management of Yellowstone set a precedent for the National Park Service, which was signed into being by Woodrow Wilson on August 25, 1916 (National Park Service, 2017).

Questions

40. This American steel magnate wrote an essay about philanthropy in 1889 that's commonly known as "The Gospel of Wealth."
    a. Hearst
    b. Carnegie
    c. Bezos
    d. Getty
41. Congress passed The Volstead Act in 1919, paving the way for the enforcement of this law.
    a. Emancipation
    b. Primogeniture
    c. Prohibition
    d. Toleration
42. The Volstead Act proved unenforceable in any real way, and in fact directly led to a rise in organized crime in the United States, so it was repealed with…
    a. 19th Amendment
    b. 21st Amendment
    c. Booze Act
    d. Medicinal Alcohol Act
43. In 1917, President Wilson cited Germany's submarine attacks on passenger and merchant ships and *this* as reasons for entering World War I against them.
    a. An insult to his mother.
    b. Germany's attempts to convince Mexico to ally with it against the US.
    c. Austria-Hungary's threats of guerilla warfare.
    d. Domestic terrorism.
44. On August 18, 1920, the 19th Amendment granted this to all citizens, regardless of sex or gender.
    a. The right to vote.
    b. The right to property.
    c. The right to choose their own religion.
    d. The right to wear pants.
45. This term was first used in 1935 to describe dust storms and drought that were sapping life from the western plains of the United States.
    a. Tornado Alley
    b. The Tin Pan
    c. The Dust Bowl
    d. The Lake
46. Franklin D. Roosevelt was elected during the Great Depression in 1933; this package of government-run social programs was his answer to it.
    a. AAA
    b. The Fireside Chats
    c. The New Deal
    d. The Youth Corp
47. This top secret project during World War II led to the creation of the atomic bomb—two of which were dropped on Japan in 1945, ending the war and causing mass destruction.
    a. The Manhattan Project
    b. The Manchurian Candidate
    c. Enola Gay
    d. Project MKUltra

Answers

40. **B. Carnegie.** Andrew Carnegie suggested in this article that it was the duty of the rich to redistribute their surplus wealth for the betterment of society rather than spending it extravagantly on themselves. It seems hypocritical of him when one looks at his career as a steel magnate, where his company brutally repressed attempts at worker organization more than once, but in the second half of his life he seemed to be attempting to make up for it by giving away the lion's share of his fortune—particularly on libraries (Standiford, 2010).
41. **C. Prohibition.** Largely prompted by temperance groups that protested the negative effects of drinking on the family, the 1919 18th Amendment to the Constitution banned the making, transport, and sale of alcoholic beverages in the United States (History.com Editors, 2019d).
42. **B. 21st Amendment.** On December 5, 1933, Prohibition was repealed entirely at the federal level. This is why liquor laws are so different from state-to-state to this very day, because each state was permitted to decide whether it would enact its own prohibition or not, and what that would look like.
43. **B. Germany's attempts to convince Mexico to ally with it against the US.** Between the naval attacks in the Mediterranean and North Atlantic, and the threat of an enemy on its southern border, the United States decided Germany was enough of a threat at home to enter the conflict (Office of the Historian, 2019).
44. **A. The right to vote.** Finally, women in the United States could cast their own vote rather than having to indirectly influence politics via the men in their lives. The last state to ratify the amendment was Tennessee (Bomboy, 2021).
45. **C. The Dust Bowl.** After a market crash in 1929, which sent the American economy reeling, droughts and bad soil conservation practices left the south-central united states reeling. The Great Depression loomed large over the 1930s.
46. **C. The New Deal.** When the first New Deal package wasn't enough to pull the economy out of the basement, Roosevelt instituted the second, more aggressive New Deal in 1935 (History.com Editors, 2009e).
47. **A. The Manhattan Project.** The idea behind the Manhattan project was that Germany would stop at nothing to create this ultimate weapon—so the United States had better beat them to it. It was with mixed feelings that the scientists on the project saw the first American atomic bomb test go off successfully, knowing they'd unleashed a technology that could destroy the world (Metcalfe, 2023).

Questions

48. The American Civil Rights Movement of these two decades sought to equalize the treatment of white people and people of color by both institutions and individuals.
    a. 1890s and 1900s
    b. 1910s and '20s
    c. 1980s and '90s
    d. 1950s and '60s
49. In 1969, this NASA mission was the first to put not just Americans but any human beings on the moon.
    a. Enterprise
    b. Mariner 4
    c. Apollo 11
    d. Voyager
50. On September 11, 2001, terrorists hijacked passenger planes and flew them into both towers of this complex in Manhattan, making this…
    a. The Sears Tower
    b. The World Trade Center
    c. The 30 Rockefeller Plaza
    d. The Empire State Building

Answers

48. **D. The 1950s and '60s.** In the wake of the Reconstruction Amendments, southern states kicked back with "Jim Crow" laws meant to restrict the rights of black Americans, and some northern states adopted policies that marginalized and endangered them. The Civil Rights movement was a massive attempt to write those continued wrongs and heal those deep cultural wounds (History.com editors, 2009a).
49. **C. Apollo 11.** On July 20, 1969, millions of Americans watched as Neil Armstrong and Buzz Aldrin took the first human walk on the moon. It lasted 3 hours and was televised all over the world, changing the way we look at our solar system forever (Watt, 2019).
50. **B. The World Trade Center.** There were two other planes: one that crashed into one side of the Pentagon in Arlington, VA, the nerve center of the US military, and another that crash-landed near Pittsburgh, PA, before reaching its target, thanks to the valiant efforts of passengers and crew (History.com Editors, 2018v).

Chapter 8:

Vive la Résistance: Revolutionaries of the World

Earth-shaking revolutions aren't particular to the United States of America. All over the world, revolutionary thinkers have stood up for their rights, the rights of the downtrodden, and even the rights of the ruling classes to rule, depending on the circumstances. All revolutionaries aren't underdogs, even if underdogs make for the best stories.

All revolutions don't have a happy ending, either, as we'll discover. While each revolutionary leader we'll explore in this chapter felt they were doing something wonderful for their people, sometimes it didn't work out the way they expected. Sometimes they were unfairly demonized by history and sometimes they were lionized when they really hadn't done much. In some cases, they were even destroyed by the revolutions they had set in motion.

Human history is all about change, and yet humans tend to fear change. Perhaps that's why revolutions have historically been more violent than not; fear and violence are often found in the same place. In this chapter, we aim not to judge, but to look at historical revolutionaries and their contributions to change—both in their times and in our own.

Questions

1. This first king of the Neo-Babylonian or Chaldean Empire (626–539 B.C.) led an uprising against the Assyrian Empire that won him the throne.
    a. Nabopolassar
    b. Ashurnasirpal II
    c. Charlamagne
    d. Hammurabi
2. Though we don't know his real name, this Gladiator led a famous slave uprising and subsequent war on Rome in 73 B.C.
    a. Helios
    b. Spartacus
    c. Nasir
    d. Crassus
3. This Roman woman and wife of Mark Antony was deeply entangled in political events following the Assassination of Julius Caesar in 44 B.C.
    a. Fulvia
    b. Hypatia
    c. Agrippina
    d. Calpurnia
4. This queen of the Celtic Iceni people in Britain led a revolt against Roman invaders in the year 60.
    a. Hannibal
    b. Emma
    c. Aethelflaed
    d. Boudica
5. This medieval Scottish rebel fought back against English King Edward I's control during the First War of Scottish Independence in 1296.
    a. William Wallace
    b. James I
    c. Robin Hood
    d. Rob Roy
6. This woman, later canonized by the Catholic Church, led French forces to victory against the English at the Siege of Orléans in 1429.
    a. Eleanor of Aquitaine
    b. Joan of Navarre
    c. Joan of Arc
    d. Teresa of Avila
7. This protestant-minded Queen of England was raised in the reformation-friendly court of Margaret of Austria, in the Netherlands, and then the French courts of Louis XII and his successor, Francis I, where the protestant reformation was gathering steam.
    a. Eleanor of Aquitaine
    b. Anne Boleyn
    c. Elizabeth I
    d. Mary of Teck
8. This English Catholic revolutionary was part of a plot to blow up James I's Parliament on November 5, 1605.
    a. Francis Bacon
    b. Percy Shelley
    c. Charles Dickens
    d. Guy Fawkes

Answers

1. **A. Nabopolassar.** While his aim was only to restore independence to Babylonia, his revolution ended up setting in motion the collapse of the entire Assyrian Empire (Gill, 2020).
2. **B. Spartacus.** A Thracian by birth, Spartacus served in the Roman army for a time before either deserting or escaping, and then being captured and sold as a slave. His uprising started in the house and gladiatorial school of his master in Capua (Editors of Encyclopedia Britannica, 2019b).
3. **A. Fulvia.** While Antony was in Egypt, Fulvia fomented rebellion against her husband's co-ruler, Octavian. Antony at least knew of her actions, though when she was defeated and sent into exile, he pretended he had not (Editors of Encyclopaedia Britannica, 2019a).
4. **D. Boudica.** After the death of her husband, King Prasutagas, who'd been allowed to operate as a Roman vassal, the Romans humiliated Boudica and her daughters publicly. In response, she led a multi-tribe revolution that defeated the Ninth Legion and destroyed Roman settlements in Britain (Pruitt, 2018).
5. **A. William Wallace.** Once he was finally betrayed and handed over to the English in 1305, Wallace was tried for treason against King Edward I of England. His reply: "I could not be a traitor to Edward, for I was never his subject." (Milligan, 2022).
6. **C. Joan of Arc.** Raised on a farm near contested territory, Joan believed she heard the voices of St. Michael, St. Catherine of Alexandria, and St. Margaret of Antioch, saying that she would deliver the French from the English. The dauphin, who had not been crowned Charles VII yet, at least accepted her as a symbol and inspiration, whether he believed her or not (Lanhers & Vale, 2023).
7. **B. Anne Boleyn.** With her father, Thomas, on diplomatic service for Henry VIII, he made sure his daughter had excellent postings so she could expand her education. When she returned to England in 1522, Anne brought her radical protestant ideas with her—and into her relationship with Henry (Nolan, 2019).
8. **D. Guy Fawkes.** Due to the treatment of English Catholics under James I and his predecessor, Elizabeth I, Fawkes planned to blow up Parliament while his comrades-in-arms started an uprising and kidnapped James I's daughter to make her a Catholic puppet queen. The plot was foiled before the fuse was lit, however—and no one knows for sure who wrote the letter that betrayed it (Greenspan, 2012).

Questions

9. This Puritan English revolutionary started his career in Parliament, then became a military leader during the English Civil Wars, then Lord Protector after the execution of Charles I.
    a. William Wallace
    b. Oliver Cromwell
    c. Thomas Cranmer
    d. Charles Stuart
10. This Swiss-born French writer was one of the post-Enlightenment thinkers that inspired French Revolutionaries with his republican ideas about *The Social Contract.*
    a. Jean-Paul Marat
    b. Eduard Manet
    c. Eugène Delacroix
    d. Jean-Jacques Rousseau
11. This French revolutionary is often blamed for the period of indiscriminate executions of unproven "enemies of the revolution" called the Reign of Terror during the French Revolution.
    a. Maximilien Robespierre
    b. Victor Hugo
    c. Jacques-François Blondel
    d. Alexandre Dumas
12. This American "founding father" from Philadelphia wasn't just a pro-revolutionary politician, but also an inventor, ambassador, and writer of pithy aphorisms.
    a. Patrick Henry
    b. Alexander Hamilton
    c. George Washington
    d. Benjamin Franklin
13. This French revolutionary aligned with the more moderate Girondin faction, and so she took it upon herself to assassinate one of the most outspoken of the more radical Jacobin faction, Jean-Paul Marat.
    a. Charlotte Corday
    b. Berthe Morisot
    c. Madame de Sévigné
    d. Simone de Beauvoir
14. This English activist is most famous for writing 1792's rationalist feminist masterpiece *A Vindication of the Rights of Woman.*
    a. Virginia Woolf
    b. Mary Wollstonecraft
    c. Olympe de Gouges
    d. Simone de Beauvoir
15. This American General and President had a surprising first career: a surveyor in 1700s Virginia.
    a. Thomas Jefferson
    b. Thomas Paine
    c. George Washington
    d. Alexander Hamilton
16. This English-born American wrote and published the first pamphlet to openly endorse American Independence, *Common Sense.*
    a. Washington Irving
    b. Thomas Paine
    c. Benjamin Franklin
    d. Jonathan Swift

Answers

9. **B. Oliver Cromwell.** After brutal campaigns in Ireland and Scotland, Cromwell was made Lord Protector for life—though he refused the title of King. After his death, the monarchy was restored to Charles II (History.com Editors, 2019m).
10. **D. Jean-Jacques Rousseau.** Though he died before the French Revolution began in 1789, his contributions to progressive republican values and strong individual morals made him a formative read for many of those who did.
11. **A. Maximilien Robespierre.** On July 28, 1794, Robespierre was guillotined with 21 of his supporters in the Revolutionary government, forever to shoulder the blame for *la Terreur*. While he certainly played a part in it, he was by no means the only actor on that stage (BBC, 2014).
12. **D. Benjamin Franklin.** As ambassador to France, Franklin convinced Louis XVI and his aristocratic court to support the American colonies' bid for freedom from England. He was famous for playing up the idea of the rustic American that the French court loved so much. He also invented bifocals and the lightning rod and started the first fire brigade in America, the Union Fire Company.
13. **A. Charlotte Corday.** She famously talked her way into his quarters (no one is exactly sure how) and was allowed in to speak with him while he was in the bath—which he did daily for a painful skin condition. She stabbed him, killing him instantly, and was arrested on the spot (Spencer, n.d.).
14. **B. Mary Wollstonecraft.** In the *Vindication*, Wollstonecraft argued that the current educational system taught girls and women to be frivolous and dependent on others for their entire life. She was a champion of equal education for the sexes (Editors of Encyclopedia Britannica, 2018a).
15. **C. George Washington.** His first professional job as a surveyor came in 1747, when he got a commission to survey Culpeper County in Western Virginia. Life as a surveyor taught the comfortably well-off Washington how to sleep and survive in the wild—which came in handy during his days with the army (Mount Vernon Ladies Association, 2023).
16. **B. Thomas Paine.** After the American Revolution, he moved to support the French Revolution, composing the iconic *Rights of Man* in defense of its principles and aims.

Questions

17. This American First Lady was an outspoken abolitionist and advocate for women's rights, as well as being wife to one and mother to another president.
    a. Abigail Adams
    b. Martha Washington
    c. Louisa Adams
    d. Martha Jefferson
18. This future emperor rose through the ranks of the revolutionary military—until he finally seized power for himself in 1799, effectively ending the French Revolution.
    a. Charles I
    b. Francis II
    c. Napoleon I
    d. Edward III
19. This farmer, General, and former enslaved person was a free man for 15 years before he went to war to overthrow colonial rule in modern-day Haiti.
    a. Toussaint L'ouverture
    b. Alexandre Pétion
    c. Alexandre Dumas
    d. Jean Price-Mars
20. This future president was the primary author of America's *Declaration of Independence* in 1776.
    a. William Henry Harrison
    b. John Hancock
    c. Samuel Adams
    d. Thomas Jefferson
21. This Venezuelan was educated both at home and in Europe, where revolutionary ideas took hold and convinced him that Latin America was ready for independence from Spain.
    a. Simón Bolívar
    b. Juan José Arévalo
    c. Eduardo Blanco
    d. Hercules Mulligan
22. This French nobleman fought for George Washington's continental army in the American Revolution before returning home to serve France in its own revolution and well beyond.
    a. Charles du Gaulle
    b. Marquis de Lafayette
    c. Pierre L'Enfant
    d. Charles Martel
23. This freedom fighter met her husband while he was an exiled mercenary in Brazil, where she took an active, armed role in the fighting. She then followed him to his home country of Italy, which they would eventually help to unite.
    a. Anita Garibaldi
    b. Mercedes Marín
    c. Manuela Sáenz
    d. Paixão Pagu
24. This revolutionary thinker is best known for his works *Das Kapital* and *The Communist Manifesto.*
    a. Arthur Schopenhauer
    b. Friedrich Schiller
    c. Alexander Gottlieb Baumgarten
    d. Karl Marx

Answers

17. **A. Abigail Adams.** Apart from her unmatched political and diplomatic clout, Adams also kept the family farm in Braintree running, raised 5 children, and kept up a lively intellectual correspondence with her husband and many of the leading minds of the American Revolution (Michals, 2015).
18. **C. Napoleon I.** Born on the island of Corsica, Napoleon Bonaparte was audacious, strategic, and ruthless in battle—and in spite of being insecure and thin-skinned, he convinced most of Europe he was the man to lead (History.com Editors, 2009o).
19. **A. Toussaint L'overture.** He first entered the war as a physician, but quickly became a respected leader, leading his people with military victories and a canny sense of how to play warring European factions off each other. He conquered the Spanish side of the island and united its halves (Willis, 2021).
20. **D. Thomas Jefferson.** A delegate to the Continental Congress in Philadelphia from his home state of Virginia, Jefferson was famously eloquent, brilliant, genteel, and educated in his day. He was also a man of deep contradictions, who was simultaneously aware that American chattel slavery was morally wrong, but was unable to support himself and his family in the style he wanted without it.
21. **A. Simón Bolívar.** He went on to play instrumental roles in the liberation of territories that became modern-day Colombia, Peru, Venezuela, Ecuador, and, of course, Bolivia (Masur, 2019).
22. **B. Marquis de Lafayette.** Marie-Joseph-Paul-Yves-Roch-Gilbert du Motier de La Fayette met the English King George III's estranged younger brother at a dinner party in 1775. He was so convincing about the wrongness of George III's policies and the genius of the intrepid Americans that Lafayette—who had no combat experience—went directly to America to fight the English (Klein, 2018).
23. **A. Anita Garibaldi.** Due to her fighting for independence in both her own country of Brazil and her husband's Italy—oftentimes while pregnant—Anita is known as a hero of two worlds, like Lafayette (Giovinazzo, 2020).
24. **D. Karl Marx.** Today, he lends his name to an economic and social theory that he hoped would serve as an equalizing, utopian alternative to Capitalism: Marxism (McLellan & Chambre, 2018).

Questions

25. This Filipino revolutionary's first novel, *Noli Me Tangere (Touch Me Not/The Social Cancer*) dealt unflinchingly with the dark side of Spanish rule in the Philippines.
    a. José Rizal
    b. Cesar Chavez
    c. Emilio Aguinaldo
    d. Rodrigo Duterte
26. This 19th century American women's rights, abolition, and temperance activist was inspired by the Quaker belief that all humans are equal in the eyes of God.
    a. Wilhelmina Drucker
    b. Bessie Parkes
    c. Susan B. Anthony
    d. Sojourner Truth
27. Near the end of Qing-era China (early 20th century), this revolutionary woman butted heads with the hyper-restrictive Confucian patriarchy through her poetry, crossdressing, swordplay, and wine-drinking.
    a. Empress Wu
    b. Qiu Jin
    c. Yang Yuhuan
    d. Empress Cixi
28. At first, this Mexican revolutionary fought with Pancho Villa's División del Norte as a man. But eventually, she revealed that she was a woman, and continued to lead her division into battle as their captain.
    a. Gabriela Mistral
    b. Jovita Idar
    c. Petra Herrera
    d. Juana Inés de la Cruz
29. This Polish-Jewish philosopher and activist wrote widely on social revolution, workers rights, and Marxism throughout WWI and the Bolshevik revolution.
    a. Hedy Lamarr
    b. Rosa Luxemburg
    c. Ernestine Rose
    d. Emma Lazarus
30. In the Irish War of Independence (1919–1921), this revolutionary gained a reputation for his decisive guerilla warfare strategy against the British—all while shouldering much of the responsibility of the Irish Elected President de Valera and Vice President Griffith while they were in jail.
    a. Michael Collins
    b. Edmund Burke
    c. Michael Joseph O'Rahilly
    d. Ernest Thomas Sinton Walton
31. This Russian revolutionary leader is known by his pseudonym; he was born Vladimir Ilich Ulyanov.
    a. Josef Stalin
    b. Mikhail Gorbechav
    c. Maxim Gorky
    d. Vladimir Lenin

Answers

25. **A. José Rizal.** Although Rizal supported strictly peaceful means of reforming Spanish colonial rule, he was arrested and, on December 30, 1896, executed in Manila. He's been an icon of independence ever since.
26. **C. Susan B. Anthony.** Though she later sullied her reputation somewhat by being against the 14th and 15 Amendments to the American Constitution that would give black men the right to vote, she claimed her objection was that women weren't included (Hayward, 2018).
27. **B. Qiu Jin.** She left her family and studied in Japan, where women had more freedom to become educated. When she returned, she opened a school for training young revolutionaries. She was soon beheaded for conspiring against the Qing government (Qin, 2018).
28. **C. Petra Herrera.** In spite of the lack of acknowledgment for women soldiers (*Soldaderas*) in the army, she carried on fighting, even becoming a spy later in her career (White, 2022).
29. **B. Rosa Luxemburg.** As much as she was a Marxist, Luxembourg disagreed vehemently with Lenin's democratic centralism, which ensured that all members of the party toed the line after an issue was decided. She was a staunch democrat (Starke, 2019).
30. **A. Michael Collins.** He was Director of Intelligence for the Irish Republican Army before being sent with Griffith to negotiate a final treaty with the British in December, 1921. The treaty was unpopular in Ireland, however, and Collins was assassinated the next year. (Editors of Encyclopaedia Britannica, 2019c).
31. **D. Vladimir Lenin.** Germany returned the exiled Lenin to Russia in 1917, hoping he'd further destabilize the current Russian regime, which was already dealing with their own revolution. It worked, and his Bolshevik party seized power (History.com Editors, 2022b).

Questions

32. This activist founded the Women's Social and Political Union (WSPU) in her effort to gain suffrage for all British women.
    a. Susan B. Anthony
    b. Emmeline Parkhurst
    c. Annie Besant
    d. Claudia Jones
33. This Russian leader of the October Revolution was Lenin's right hand man through the Russian Civil War and WWI.
    a. Leon Trotsky
    b. Anatoly Lunacharsky
    c. Konstantin Pysin
    d. Leo Tolstoy
34. This German student was arrested, along with her brother and other close friends, for distributing anti-Nazi pamphlets at the University of Munich in in 1943.
    a. Marlene Dietrich
    b. Anne Frank
    c. Sophie Scholl
    d. Amalie Emmy Noether
35. Using his skills as a lawyer and commitment to the principle of pacifism, this Indian revolutionary successfully organized grassroots resistance to British colonial rule.
    a. R.K. Narayan
    b. Mahatma Gandhi
    c. Rabindranath Tagore
    d. Chandragupta Maurya
36. This yogi, philosopher, and Indian nationalist revolutionary was the first Indian political figure to publicly suggest that India should be totally independent from the British Empire.
    a. Sri Aurobindo
    b. Swami Vivekananda
    c. Vikram Sarabhai
    d. Satyajit Ray
37. This activist not only helped to pen the Indian constitution, but overcame immense societal discrimination as a Dalit, or person of a depressed caste, in a time when they were still considered "untouchable."
    a. Swami Vivekananda
    b. Satendra Singh
    c. B.R. Ambedkar
    d. Arundhati Roy
38. This conflicted revolutionary served as the first ever Prime Minister of the Democratic Republic of the Congo once Belgium pulled out.
    a. Nelson Mandela
    b. Patrice Lumumba
    c. Sukarno
    d. François Luambo
39. This American civil rights activist found the teachings of the Nation of Islam while in jail and came out the other side a minister on a mission.
    a. John Lewis
    b. Rosa Parks
    c. Bayard Rustin
    d. Malcolm X

Answers

32. **B. Emmeline Parkhurst.** She was put in jail along with other members for revolutionary actions that included arson, but they called off the fight for suffrage temporarily at the start of WWI (Editors of Encyclopedia Britannica, 2019a).
33. **A. Leon Trotsky.** After Lenin died, Josef Stalin began a massive propaganda campaign to leave Trotsky in the dust. Trotsky spoke out against Stalin's brutal regime from abroad until he was assassinated by their agents in 1940 (Daniels, 2023).
34. **C. Sophie Scholl.** Sophie and her brother Hans were arrested on the spot. Though they were questioned and subjected to a Nazi show trial, they never gave up the rest of their friends in their small resistance group, the White Rose. Her bravery is honored in Germany to this day (Hill, 2021).
35. **B. Mahatma Gandhi.** Born Mohandas Karamchand Gandhi in Porbandar, Gujarat, the man later known as the Mahatma—or *great soul*—first used his technique of passive resistance in response to racism in South Africa. When he returned to India, he used his non-cooperation strategy to help India gain independence (History.com Editors, 2010f).
36. **A. Sri Aurobindo.** His Calcutta newspaper, *Bande Mataram*, was a mouthpiece for early Indian nationalist sentiment. Later, he founded his ashram or monastery in Pondicherry, where people can still experience his Integral Yoga to this day (Sri Aurobindo Ashram, n.d.).
37. **C. B.R. Ambedkar.** He fought for education and self-respect for all Indians, looking at his newly independent country through the lens of social justice and equality. As an adult, Ambedkar converted from Hinduism to Buddhism, finding its tenants much more palatable considering his long and arduous fight against the Hindu-based caste system in India (Tharoor, 2023).
38. **B. Patrice Lumumba.** Lumumba was assassinated young, partly due to US fears that he'd ally with Russia, partly because the Belgian authorities didn't trust him, and partly because he was out of favor with elements of his own government (Cordell, 2019).
39. **D. Malcolm X.** After becoming disenchanted with the Nation of Islam's leadership and taking his own pilgrimage to Mecca, Malcolm X came back to the US and started the Organization of Afro-American Unity, where his new, more moderate ideas gained even more traction (History.com Editors, 2009d).

Questions

40. This Argentine-born Marxist was drawn to the Cuban anti-dictator cause in 1955 when he met Fidel Castro and became his right-hand man.
    a. Ché Guevara
    b. Nikita Khruschev
    c. José de San Martín
    d. Manuel Belgrano
41. This minister and civil rights activist had his first experience organizing a large-scale protest with the Montgomery Bus Boycott, which was inspired by Rosa Parks's refusal to sit in the segregated back section of a public bus.
    a. Bayard Rustin
    b. Martin Luther King, Jr.
    c. Jacob Lawrence
    d. William Grant Still
42. In Vietnam, this man and his communist Viet Minh party seized the opportunity to take their country back when Japan surrendered to the United States in 1945.
    a. Dien Bien Phu
    b. Le Duc Tho
    c. Ho Chi Minh
    d. Trung Trac
43. This Indonesian nationalist was at the forefront of his country's struggle to achieve independence from Dutch colonial rule.
    a. Sukarno
    b. Pramoedya Ananta Toer
    c. Achmad Soebardjo
    d. Hayam Wuruk
44. This revolutionary was responsible for the disastrous "Great Leap Forward" and the Chinese Cultural Revolution.
    a. Ho Chi Minh
    b. Mao Zedong
    c. Sun Yat-sen
    d. Deng Xiaoping
45. This "Father of modern Angola" was a medical doctor and poet as well as the first president of the People's Republic of Angola.
    a. Agostinho Neto
    b. Viriato da Cruz
    c. Pepetela
    d. Álvaro Holden Roberto
46. After the Shah's pro-Western government collapsed, this religious leader and politician, formerly in exile, returned to make Iran the world's first Islamic republic.
    a. Muammar Gaddafi
    b. Anwar Sadat
    c. Ruhollah Khomeini
    d. Gamal Abdel Nasser
47. This poet laureate and first president of independent Senegal spent time in a Nazi concentration camp. He joined the French resistance movement when released.
    a. Wasis Diop
    b. Léopold Senghor
    c. Mamadou Dia
    d. Muammar Gaddafi

Answers

40. **A. Ché Guevara.** Ernesto Guevara de la Serna proved a wonderful leader for the Cuban revolution, if not a very good administrator. He went on to promote independence all over South America, eventually being captured and killed in Bolivia in 1967.
41. **B. Martin Luther King, Jr.** He continued to be integral to, if not the face of, the American civil rights movement in the '60s. He also denounced America's involvement with the Vietnam war, in part thanks to a friendship with Buddhist luminary Thitch Nhat Hanh. At 35, MLK became the youngest man to ever win the Nobel Peace Prize. He was assassinated on April 4, 1968 (The Nobel Prize, 2018).
42. **C. Ho Chi Minh.** France, who'd been run out by Japan years earlier, refused to recognize Vietnamese independence; Vietnam partitioned, with Ho ruling North Vietnam and the US-backed Ngo Dinh Diem in the South, eventually leading to the Vietnam War (Editors of Encyclopaedia Britannica, 2003).
43. **A. Sukarno.** He served as an advisor to the Japanese during their occupation in WWII, but once Japan surrendered he declared Indonesian independence. The Dutch finally officially ceded control in 1949 (Hanna, 2018).
44. **B. Mao Zedong.** On 1 October 1949, Mao declared The People's Republic of China. Radical economic, agricultural, and social reforms followed (BBC, 2014a).
45. **A. Agostinho Neto.** His Movimento Popular de Libertação de Angola (MPLA) was one of three factions vying for power after Portugal pulled out in 1975. With the help of Cuban forces, Neto triumphed (Editors of Encyclopaedia Britannica, 2023d).
46. **C. Ruhollah Khomeini.** In his early years, Khomeini's religious studies got him the title of ayatollah, which is given to leading scholars in Shi'ite theology and law. His legacy is a controversial one today (BBC, 2014b).
47. **B. Léopold Senghor.** As president, he was a great proponent of fair trade, the African cultural movement known as Negritude, diplomatic relationships with other African countries, and continued cooperation with France (Editors of Encyclopaedia Britannica, 2019b).

Questions

48. This Tibetan nun led guerilla fighter resistance in the Himalayas in the '50s and '60s, then spent 21 years in a Chinese prison before finally being released.
    a. Bhrikuti Devi
    b. Ani Pachen Dolma
    c. Yeshe Tsogyal
    d. Ma Drag Sinmo
49. This first black president of South Africa served 27 years in prison for his outspoken opposition to his country's racial apartheid system.
    a. Nelson Mandela
    b. Barack Obama
    c. Desmond Tutu
    d. Walter Sisulu
50. This Zimbabwean president and prime minister is revered for bringing independence to his country and fighting neocolonialism.
    a. Desmond Tutu
    b. Gamal Abdel Nasser
    c. Robert Mugabe
    d. Canaan Banana

Answers

48. **B. Ani Pachen Dolma.** After her release, Ani Pachen led protests against Chinese atrocities in Lhasa, before she was forced to escape to Nepal—on foot—under threat of arrest again (Donnelley, 2002).
49. **A. Nelson Mandela.** In 1993, before he was elected, Mandela and then-president F.W. de Klerk won the Nobel Peace Prize for transitioning South Africa out of apartheid. Mandela became president in 1994 (Augustyn, 2018).
50. **C. Robert Mugabe.** He was in power for 37 years, but his administration later became corrupt and ruthless, tainting his legacy for some in Zimbabwe around the world (Winter, 2019).

Chapter 9:

Global Theaters: The Great World Wars

War has been a constant of human civilization throughout our history. Where we find one wealthy city or town, we'll find another who thinks they're more deserving of that wealth. Humans have blamed our tendency for war on gods, on legends, on grudges, on family feuds, on personal insults real and perceived. War was considered the last recourse but also a necessary thing. It would be more shameful for a ruler *not* to defend themselves and their people, after all.

The World Wars were different, though. Thanks to improvements in rail and ocean transport, the world had become much smaller in the decades before WWI. Territorial disputes were nothing new in Europe, but in this new war, the level of connection between the involved states and their empires, plus the deadly advances made in weapons technology in the preceding century upped the ante. The horrific slog of trench warfare was explored to its fullest; shell shock brought attention at long last to the trauma of war; and some even say that many countries, America included, lost their innocence in the fight. War was dialed up to 11, and no one was safe.

Even as WWI came to an end, the seeds for WWII were sown. Distrust, disenfranchisement, and old hurts found an outlet in new hatreds. Much of the world suffered for it, as fear led to blame, and blame led to mass murder on a scale never before seen in the world. But the lessons of these wars are some of the most important ones history has for us, lest we should be tempted to repeat the mistakes that led to all that death and destruction in the first place.

On that somber note, let's jump into the biggest conflicts of the 20th century, one after the other.

Questions

1. The assassination of Archduke Franz Ferdinand and the Duchess of Hohenberg in this city in 1914 is generally considered the inciting incident of WWI or The Great War.
    a. Vienna
    b. Sarajevo
    c. Budapest
    d. Prague
2. Austria-Hungary declared war on Serbia after this assassination in 1914, and Germany declared war on this major power around the same time, citing their perceived battle-readiness against their Austro-Hungarian allies.
    a. The United States
    b. Russia
    c. China
    d. Singapore
3. Seeing their greatest enemy Russia preparing for war, this Ottoman-ruled country allied with Germany for mutual defense in 1914.
    a. India
    b. Morocco
    c. Turkey
    d. New Guinea
4. Although Belgium had declared neutrality, German troops advanced on this Belgian city and besieged it, making it the site of the first battle of WWI.
    a. Bruges
    b. Amsterdam
    c. Warsaw
    d. Liège
5. The first shot in the Asian Pacific theater during WWI was fired at the *SS Pfaltz*, a German merchant ship, moments after this allied Pacific nation learned that England was at war.
    a. Australia
    b. New Zealand
    c. Trinidad and Tobago
    d. Japan
6. To weaken Germany's hold on its empire, Britain and France invaded their colonies in Africa. They saw immediate success with this campaign in West Africa.
    a. Somalia
    b. Senegal
    c. Togoland
    d. Congo
7. This British ally in the Pacific secured shipping channels and led a joint operation to defeat German forces in Tsingtao, China.
    a. Singapore
    b. Japan
    c. New Zealand
    d. Sri Lanka
8. On September 1, 1914, St. Petersburg (*Sankt Peterburg*) was renamed this—to get rid of the German word "sankt" and suffix of "burg."
    a. Leningrad
    b. Petrograd
    c. Moscow
    d. Nizhny Novgorod

Answers

1. **B. Sarajevo.** The Archduke, who was heir to the Austro-Hungarian throne, and his wife had just narrowly avoided a bomb tossed their way hours before they were gunned down by the 18-year-old Bosnian-Serb nationalist, Gavrilo Princip (Saelee, 2023).
2. **B. Russia.** After the assassination of the Archduke, Serbia requested help from Russia to stave off both Austro-Hungarian reprisals and threats to take Serbia altogether. Germany, allied with Austria-Hungary, responded to the threat with their allies (Castelow, 2017).
3. **C. Turkey.** Turkey's Minister for War, Enver Pasha, signed a secret defense treaty with Germany in August, 1914. Although Prime Minister Sait Halim wanted to remain neutral, Pasha's viewpoint won out eventually (Ministry for Culture and Heritage, 2014).
4. **D. Liège.** The German army started their assault on August 5. Due to brave resistance, led by King Albert himself, it took 10 days and the literal big guns—massive German siege cannons—to take the city. (History.com Editors, 2009s).
5. **A. Australia.** The *Pfaltz* was converted to a troop transport ship and renamed *HMAT Boorara*, in service with the Australian Imperial Force for the rest of the war (Other, 2014).
6. **C. Togoland.** German forces in Togo tried to resist, but most of Germany's attention was focused on its European campaign just then—some cities didn't even put up a fight when the French and British came (The National Archives, 2015).
7. **B. Japan.** Joint Japanese-Anglo efforts to tamp down German influence in the Pacific were largely successful, and Japan acquired several German possessions for itself in the process (Kiilleen, 2017).
8. **B. Petrograd.** Petro still honored Peter the Great, who'd envisioned and created the city before naming it after himself, and used the Russian suffix "-grad" to change its name to the Russian version of Peter's City. Later, the city would be renamed Leningrad after Vladimir Lenin, then return to being St. Petersburg again after Lenin's death in 1924 (Rosenberg, 2023).

Questions

9. The British Secret Service Bureau got its start in 1909 with a mission to uncover an extensive spy network of German nationals operating in England during WWI. Later, it was divided into *this* (MI5) and The Secret Intelligence Service (MI6).
    a. The Foreign Office
    b. Ministry of War
    c. Scotland Yard
    d. The Security Service
10. The modern use of trench warfare and these kinds of weapons, later banned by the Geneva Protocol of 1925, occurred in the European theater of WWI.
    a. Nuclear
    b. Chemical
    c. Tank
    d. Biological
11. A German U-Boat sank this luxury passenger liner on 7 May 1915. The international outcry was so loud that a few months later, Germany halted unrestricted submarine warfare.
    a. RMS Titanic
    b. RMS Campania
    c. RMS Lusitania
    d. RMS Majestic
12. When war broke out and the Germans invaded Belgium, British Nurse Edith Cavell raced back to her post at a teaching hospital, soon to be a Red Cross hospital, in this occupied city.
    a. Brussels
    b. Rotterdam
    c. Antwerp
    d. Ghent
13. This revolution in 1916 further weakened the Ottoman Empire's hold on modern-day Turkey.
    a. The Arab Spring
    b. The Arab Revolution
    c. The Easter Rising
    d. The Jasmine Revolution
14. The Zimmerman Telegram served as an impetus for the United States to enter WWI on the side of the allies, as it tried to convince this nearby country to ally against the US should it enter the war.
    a. Canada
    b. Colombia
    c. Brazil
    d. Mexico
15. This battle, the third of its name in Belgium or Flanders, represented the worst excesses of human life wasted that came with trench warfare.
    a. Battle of Ypres
    b. Battle of Gibraltar
    c. Battle of the Marne
    d. Battle of Bunker Hill

Answers

9. **D. The Security Service.** Winston Churchill, at the time Home Secretary in Prime Minister H. H. Asquith's cabinet, lent all the support he could to this new Intelligence agency (Andrew, n.d.).
10. **B. Chemical.** France was the first to use chemical weapons, then referred to as "Gas." They used tear gas in 1914. Germans first used chlorine gas as a weapon at Ypres in 1925. They also used carbon monoxide and Zyklon B to murder millions of people, Jews, Romani, and others, in death camps like Auschwitz (Patton, 2022).
11. **C. RMS Lusitania.** Of the 1200 civilians killed in the attack, 128 were American citizens, inciting the then-neutral United States. They didn't enter the war, but they did protest so strongly that it pushed Germany to stop making unregulated attacks in the Atlantic (Imperial War Museums, n.d.).
12. **A. Brussels.** On 5 August 1915, Cavell was arrested for helping Allied soldiers from her hospital patients escape Belgium and return home. She was tried and executed along with 34 others from her network (Imperial War Museums, 2018).
13. **B. The Arab Revolution.** Already weakened from entering the war on the German side with strained finances, the Ottoman Empire was ripe for a revolution (Ministry for Culture and Heritage, 2014b).
14. **D. Mexico.** In return for Mexico's help, if the US declared war on Germany, Germany would help Mexico reconquer New Mexico, Texas and Arizona from the US (Library of Congress, n.d.).
15. **A. Ypres.** The 3rd Battle of Ypres, also called Passchendaele, took three months to be decided. Although Canadian and British troops eventually captured the village under General Haig, it cost 310,000 British lives to 260,000 on the German side (History.com Editors, 2018s).

Questions

16. While Czar Nicholas II started off the conflict of WWI, this Revolution led by this man made sure he didn't survive to see the end of the war.
    a. The Cultural Revolution
    b. The Velvet Revolution
    c. The Bolshevik Revolution
    d. The Haitian Revolution
17. The first US offensive in WWI was over this French village near the Somme.
    a. Aix-en-Provence
    b. Cantigny
    c. Gordes
    d. Belcastel
18. This offensive, carried out from September–November of 1918 across the entire Western Front, was the deadliest military campaign in US history.
    a. TET offensive
    b. Operation Red Dawn
    c. Meuse–Argonne offensive
    d. Belgrade Offensive
19. As a result of WWI and the Bolshevik Revolution in Russia, many countries in this once-great empire began to demand independence of their own.
    a. The German Empire
    b. The Napoleonic Empire
    c. The Ottoman Empire
    d. The Austro-Hungarian Empire
20. This German Emperor, grandson to England's Queen Victoria, was forced to abdicate after the war in November, 1918.
    a. Otto I
    b. Wilhelm II
    c. Ferdinand I
    d. Frederick II
21. After four years, the guns finally went quiet not with a surrender, but with this on the Western Front at 11 o'clock on November 11, 1918.
    a. Armistice
    b. Victory Ball
    c. Log-off
    d. Summit
22. This name of confederation of Balkan states, created in the wake of the dissolution of the Austro-Hungarian Empire, literally translates to, "Land of the South Slavs."
    a. Czechoslovakia
    b. Yugoslavia
    c. Macedonia
    d. Montenegro
23. This treaty, ratified after WWI, held Germany entirely responsible for the ravages of the war.
    a. Treaty of Nantes
    b. Treaty of Versailles
    c. Treaty of Ghent
    d. Jay Treaty

Answers

16. **C. The Bolshevik Revolution.** Thanks to the failure of the Czar as a military leader and collapsing Russian infrastructure during WWI, Lenin's Bolshevik party took control of Petrograd, forced Nicholas II to abdicate, and assassinated him and his family (Kiger, 2021a).
17. **B. Cantigny.** Once the village was captured from German occupiers, American General Pershing gave the order that it was not to be surrendered under any circumstances. The 72 hours that followed until reinforcements came were exhausting (History.com Editors, 2018t).
18. **C. Meuse–Argonne offensive.** It was the primarily American part of the Hundred Days Offensive, which brought the war on the Western front to an end, finally (National Archives, 2018).
19. **D. The Austro-Hungarian Empire.** The last Habsburg Emperor, Charles I of Austria, ceded his right to political power in both Austria and Hungary in 1918. Several of the smaller countries had already broken off during the war (Royde-Smith, 2023).
20. **B. Wilhelm II.** Kaiser (Emperor) Wilhelm II was mainly a public-relations manager for Germany, and not a very good one, during the war. After it, he lived out the rest of his life in Exile in the Netherlands (History.com Editors, 2018l).
21. **A. Armistice.** Rather than a surrender, both the Central Powers and the Allies agreed to an armistice, or agreement to stop fighting. In order to push a surrender, the Allies would've had to invade Germany, and both sides were already too exhausted and depleted for that (Kiger, 2018).
22. **B. Yugoslavia.** The modern countries that were a part of this original Yugoslavia are Bosnia and Herzegovina, Croatia, Kosovo, Montenegro, North Macedonia, Serbia, and Slovenia (Wilde, 2019b).
23. **B. Treaty of Versailles.** At the Paris Peace Conference of 1919, The Big Four—The US, Britain, Italy, and France—dictated difficult terms to Germany that they had no choice but to accept (History.com Editors, 2009h).

Questions

24. This organization, focused on international cooperation, was born from the ashes of WWI.
    a. NATO
    b. The European Union
    c. INTERPOL
    d. League of Nations
25. After the war, Germany instituted a new, democratic form of government that called itself this.
    a. New Germany
    b. The Weimar Republic
    c. Oktoberfest
    d. The Frankfurt Democracy
26. The Treaty of Versailles left Germany in dire economic and political straits, which led to the public openness to the charismatic-but-hateful message of this soon-to-be-Chancellor.
    a. Adolf Hitler
    b. Rudolf Hess
    c. Heinrich Brüning
    d. Paul von Hindenburg
27. This new Chancellor's party, officially called the *Nationalsozialistische Deutsche Arbeiterpartei*, was not at all socialist—as the name implies—but very nationalist, racist, and antisemitic.
    a. Bavarian People's Party
    b. German National People's Party
    c. The Nazi Party
    d. The Centre Party
28. When Hitler's regime started making noises about war, this Soviet leader signed the German-Soviet Nonaggression Pact, in theory leaving him free to continue his policies of acquisition and tyranny.
    a. Vladimir Lenin
    b. Leon Trotsky
    c. Fyodor Dostoevsky
    d. Josef Stalin
29. Germany found common ground with this far-off country, whose government had also adopted an expansionist, nationalistic, and racist ideology, with the signing of the Anti-Comintern Pact on November 25, 1936.
    a. Korea
    b. Japan
    c. Egypt
    d. Kenya
30. On September 27, 1939, this Polish city fell to German forces after a 26 day siege. A German program of terror, mass executions, and forced displacement followed.
    a. Krakow
    b. Budapest
    c. Warsaw
    d. Gdańsk

Answers

24. **D. League of Nations.** This association was headquartered in Geneva, Switzerland, in the hope that future disputes between nations could be settled through diplomacy rather than war (Editors of Encyclopedia Britannica, 2020).
25. **B. The Weimar Republic.** Since Berlin was still in turmoil, the new capital was moved to Weimar. It used a system of proportional representation, wherein parties gained the number of seats proportional to the amount of votes they received (The Holocaust Explained, n.d.).
26. **A. Adolf Hitler.** This Austrian-born struggling artist fought for Germany in WWI, but only after he was tracked down in Munich for not registering for military service in the first place (Pruitt, 2019).
27. **C. The Nazi Party.** Already deeply racist before Hitler became involved, once he joined, he set about organizing the party toward the goal of promoting German supremacy, both in Europe and over humanity in general (The Wiener Holocaust Library, n.d.).
28. **D. Josef Stalin.** In 1941, Germany broke the pact and invaded the USSR, which was still struggling from famine and economic disaster brought on by Stalin's policies. While Stalin joined the Allies, where Russia was instrumental to defeating Hitler, he also continued terrorizing his own people with gulags and purges.
29. **B. Japan.** Although they seem unlikely allies due to deeply racist ideologies at the time, Japan's fear of Soviet incursions eastward and Hitler's desire to denounce Soviet Bolshevism—and communism in general—gave these two countries obsessed with their own superiority common ground (Dawsey, 2021).
30. **C. Warsaw.** Before Hitler even entered Poland, he warned that he had a special use in mind for Poland, one he didn't think he could get away with in Germany. He meant, of course, the concentration camps (History.com Editors, 2009j).

Questions

31. Though he was warned repeatedly of the German threat, Prime Minister Neville Chamberlain ignored them long enough that, once the war began, he had to resign—leaving this man to step into his shoes.
    a. Winston Churchill
    b. Franklin Delano Roosevelt
    c. Lloyd George
    d. William Gladstone
32. Operation Dynamo evacuated 338,000 British and French soldiers from certain death in this small French coastal village in the face of onrushing, overwhelming German forces.
    a. Lille
    b. Caens
    c. Dunkirk
    d. Riems
33. Hitler and the Nazi party used this euphemism to refer to the planned murder of every Jewish person within their grasp.
    a. The Countdown
    b. The Final Solution
    c. The Axis of Evil
    d. Operation Birke
34. On June 14, 1940, France fell to Germany, and Hitler's administrators set up a new puppet government in this French city, away from Paris.
    a. Lyon
    b. Calais
    c. Vichy
    d. Marseille
35. General Charles de Gaulle, who was the figurehead and leader of the French resistance against Vichy and Germany, convinced Supreme Allied Commander Dwight Eisenhower to join him in freeing this city in late August, 1944 rather than focusing resources elsewhere.
    a. Nantes
    b. Vichy
    c. Paris
    d. Dunkirk
36. The Luftwaffe or German Air Force focused on invading this island country for over 3 months during this operation, known as the Battle of…
    a. Iceland
    b. Britain
    c. Hawaii
    d. Malta
37. The failure of the German Operation Barbarossa, a campaign to invade and defeat this country, was a turning point for the Allies.
    a. USSR
    b. Poland
    c. Morocco
    d. Italy

Answers

31. **A. Winston Churchill.** Though he had a long and convoluted career as a politician, historian, writer, and military man, his early assessments of the war along with his charm and strategic ability meant he's mostly remembered for being a rather successful wartime Prime Minister.
32. **C. Dunkirk.** This evacuation, which saved the majority of Britain and France's soldiers to fight another day, also allowed Germany to annex half of France quickly. While it wasn't considered a win by the Allies, it wasn't a defeat, either (History.com Editors, 2018a).
33. **B. The Final Solution.** Aka "The Final Solution to the Jewish Problem" and the "Romani Problem" was a plan for total annihilation and genocide through invasion, mass murder, and concentration camps.
34. **C. Vichy.** Marshal Pétain became the head of the new, authoritarian French regime overseen by German interests. The Vichy government colluded in arresting and deporting Jewish people among other acts that chipped away at its public popularity over the course of the war (Boissoneault, 2017).
35. **C. Paris.** De Gaulle threatened to go into Paris with or without the other Allies, as he'd been preparing his forces in London for some time, but he finally convinced Eisenhower by suggesting they should get to Paris and beat out the communist, Soviet forces who might otherwise liberate it and skew public opinion in their direction. Well played (History.com Editors, 2018o).
36. **B. Britain.** The British Royal Air Force, along with pilots and fighters from many Allied countries, held the Luftwaffe at bay in what amounted to a major defensive victory (Imperial War Museums, 2018a).
37. **A. USSR.** Even though Stalin didn't expect the German invasion, the USSR's superior numbers, entrenched resistance, and harsh climate all eventually converged to make Operation Barbarossa a disaster for Nazi forces (History.com Editors, 2009f).

Questions

38. Before the sudden Japanese attack on this US Naval base, the United States had merely been sending aid and selling munitions to Britain without becoming fully involved in the war.
    a. San Francisco
    b. Norfolk
    c. Pearl Harbor
    d. La Jolla
39. After defeating Italian Axis forces in North Africa, the Allies turned their attention to Italy itself, initiating Operation Husky, or the invasion of this island.
    a. Corsica
    b. Crete
    c. Capri
    d. Sicily
40. Though women couldn't join the US armed forces for combat purposes, hundreds of thousands of them joined the workforce to make munitions or joined these two military auxiliaries on the front.
    a. Pink and White Ladies
    b. WAC and WASP
    c. EER and EPR
    d. MOS and OPSEC
41. Before the war, this nation was a commonwealth of the United States. After Japan invaded in 1942, American general MacArthur pledged to free it again.
    a. Bora Bora
    b. Australia
    c. Fiji
    d. Philippines
42. In July 1943, Benito Mussolini, leader of the Axis nation of fascist Italy, was deposed by a vote of his own Grand Council and taken to…
    a. The guillotine
    b. The firing squad
    c. Jail on the island of Ponza
    d. House arrest
43. 6 June 1944, better known as this, was the start of Operation Overlord, an ambitious, amphibious allied assault on German-occupied France.
    a. D-Day
    b. Bastille Day
    c. Tax Day
    d. V-E Day
44. This British colonial territory contributed the largest volunteer force in the world to the WWII Allies.
    a. Sri Lanka
    b. Hong Kong
    c. India
    d. Australia
45. After the invasion of Normandy, Allies advanced toward Germany. This battle was the last major effort the Germans made to hold them back.
    a. Battle of the Somme
    b. Battle of the Bulge
    c. Guadalcanal Campaign
    d. Battle of Crete

Answers

38. **C. Pearl Harbor.** President Roosevelt had relocated the US Pacific Fleet to Hawaii from San Diego, in case of trouble in the Pacific theater. Japan secreted their fleet toward Hawaii, bombed Pearl Harbor, and then, with the closest fleet distracted, started taking out European Ally holdings in the Pacific (Citino, 2021).
39. **D. Sicily.** Once the Allies had a jumping-off point from a secured Sicily, they set their sights on what Winston Churchill called the "soft underbelly of Europe" and Benito Mussolini (Hickman, 2023).
40. **B. WAC and WASP.** The Women's Army Corps worked both at home and abroad in non-combat jobs with full military status. The Women's Airforce Service Pilots, all of whom had a pilot's license before the war began, did logistic flights for the Airforce (History.com Editors, 2021).
41. **D. Philippines.** The loss of life was massive on both sides of the campaign in the Philippines, with Japan's Air Force practically decimated and tens of thousands of American, Filipino, Mexican, and Australian troops on the Allied side died (Vergun, 2020).
42. **C. Jail on the island of Ponza.** None of his fellow fascists came to his rescue, but German commandos did eventually, setting him up as head of one of their puppet states in Northern Italy. Once that was lost, Mussolini was captured trying to escape to Switzerland and executed in 1945 (History.com Editors, 2009r).
43. **A. D-Day.** An international effort was made to plan, supply, and execute this ambitious plan that would finally allow the Allies to get a foothold in northern Europe (Imperial War Museums, 2000).
44. **C. India.** Though India was close to gaining its own independence from Britain at this point in history, 2 million Indians volunteered to fight on the side of the Allies (Karnad, 2015).
45. **B. Battle of the Bulge.** Near the wooded plateau of Ardennes, Germany scraped up as many reinforcements as it could to throw at the Allies, hoping to drive a wedge through their lines. Though they inflicted a great deal of damage at a relatively low cost, the German forces were too depleted after the battle to withstand the Allies for long (Editors of Encyclopedia Britannica, 2018d).

Questions

46. In a time when black Americans were still denied many of their civil rights, black soldiers like these famous pilots made massive contributions to the war effort—often at great personal cost.
    a. The Flying Vs
    b. The Blue Angels
    c. Tuskegee Airmen
    d. Smarties
47. Germany surrendered unconditionally to the Allies on May 7, 1945. March 8 is celebrated every year to commemorate the end of WWII, called…
    a. Surrender Day
    b. Bastille Day
    c. Harmony Day
    d. V-E Day
48. In spite of the decimation of its armed forces and the defeat of the European Axis powers, Japan refused to surrender. Rather than send Allied forces to take Japan by force, the United States dropped its brand new atomic bomb on…
    a. Tokyo
    b. Kyoto
    c. Hiroshima
    d. Hanoi
49. In the wake of the war, the Allies convened an International Military Tribunal in this German city to put the Nazis on trial for crimes against humanity and war crimes.
    a. Berlin
    b. Nuremberg
    c. Munich
    d. Frankfurt
50. In the wake of WWII, the somewhat defunct League of Nations was replaced by this international, cooperative governing body.
    a. The Justice League
    b. NATO
    c. Axis and Allies
    d. The United Nations

Answers

46. **C. Tuskegee Airmen.** Over 1000 American airmen trained at the Tuskegee Institute in Alabama, a school started by Dr. Booker T. Washington in 1881. More than half of them saw combat in WWII (American Experience, n.d.).
47. **D. V-E Day.** Victory in Europe Day, as it's called in the UK, is still celebrated in countries who fought in WWII. Hitler had committed suicide a week before, and his successor was left to authorise the declaration of surrender (National Archives, 2021).
48. **C. Hiroshima.** After the carnage at Hiroshima on August 6, Japan's supreme war council was split on whether or not to surrender. A second horrific atomic bomb dropped on Nagasaki and a Russian invasion of Manchuria two days later forced their hands. The war was over (History.com Editors, 2019b).
49. **B. Nuremberg.** Judges from each of the 4 Allied countries heard the indictments and arguments of the 4 prosecutors, one from each nation. Of the 24 defendants, 19 were found guilty. 12 were sentenced to death (The National WWII Museum, 2023).
50. **D. United Nations.** Every country that had declared war on Germany and Japan by March, 1945, was invited to join. More countries followed in the years to come, and today it's more difficult to think of a country that *doesn't* belong (United Nations, n.d.).

Chapter 10:

Human Ingenuity: Inventors and Problem Solvers

We've talked about some of the greatest civilizations, revolutions, wars, and discoveries that fueled human ingenuity already—but there's so much more to explore. Since humans have existed, we've been inventing things. At our core, we're all problem solvers. We adapt to any terrain, any weather, any situation, even if it's outwardly hostile. We just need a few years to collect the data and create a solution. Then a few more years to test it out.

That makes it sound much simpler than it is, of course. But it is worth doing, and this chapter proves that.

This chapter is dedicated to the solutions. To the humans who saw a problem, solved it, and put their innovations out there to benefit each and every one of us. The wheel, the refrigerator, electric light, things we take for granted each and every day didn't exist when humans first walked this beautiful planet. We invented them to solve problems, to make living better, easier, more rewarding. It's what we do. Let's celebrate it.

Questions

1. The earliest period of human prehistory is named for tools made from this simple but durable material.
    a. Plastic
    b. Steel
    c. Stone
    d. Iron
2. Arguably the greatest human invention, and one absolutely essential for communication, possibly started with one proto-form 150000 years ago.
    a. Poetry
    b. Language
    c. Computers
    d. Mathematics
3. This technology, now one of humanity's most basic needs, developed about 170000 years ago and allowed the first humans to migrate away from the warmth of Africa to cooler, harsher climates.
    a. Clothing
    b. The wheel
    c. Religion
    d. Writing
4. The invention of this weapon technology allowed hunters to find their dinner more efficiently as early as 64000 years ago.
    a. Gunpowder
    b. Bow and arrow
    c. Spear
    d. Knife
5. This simple tool set, involving a cup or bowl and a club-shaped object, has been used for breaking down ingredients like grain or other plant matter for 35000 years.
    a. Harpoon and net
    b. Plough and saddle
    c. Mortar and pestle
    d. Needles and hooks
6. This technology allowed Neolithic (4300–2000 B.C.) humans to collect and store liquids effectively.
    a. Baskets
    b. Shoes
    c. Polymers
    d. Pottery
7. Although fermentation is a natural process, humans probably started purposefully making this substance about 35000 years ago.
    a. Alcohol
    b. Pickles
    c. Kimchi
    d. Psilocybin
8. This process for obtaining and strengthening metal from raw ore was probably invented around 5000 B.C. in Anatolia or modern-day Turkey.
    a. Forging
    b. Smelting
    c. Hammering
    d. Mining

Answers

1. **C. Stone.** Though the stone age is often said to last from 30000 B.C. to 3000 B.C., some modern archaeologists argue it should stretch back as far as 2.6 million years, considering evidence of tools from then. The very first tools were probably of wood or bone, things that require less force to manipulate, but also don't last as long in the fossil record (Smithsonian Institute, 2009).
2. **B. Language.** Though it's difficult to decipher, since Language is around 15000 years old but its written evidence, or writing, is only 6000, there are many theories about this possible proto-language in the academic world today (McWhorter, 2020).
3. **A. Clothing.** Though the last Ice Age was 120000 years ago, modern DNA studies have shown that humans started wearing clothing even before then, as early as 180000 years ago. Believe it or not, the DNA they tested was that of clothing lice (University of Florida, 2011).
4. **B. Bow and Arrow.** The oldest evidence of a bow and arrow comes to us from Sibudu Cave in South Africa. The arrowheads have stone tips made for piercing and show evidence of plant-based glue. The glue means that arrows were what archaeologists call composite tools, tools made from more than one part or thing, which are significantly more complex to make and operate (Gill, 2010).
5. **C. Mortar and Pestle.** Probably originating from the idea of a quern-stone and mallet, used to process grains, this handheld version is still used to this day in kitchens and pharmacies around the world.
6. **D. Pottery.** 10000 years ago, the first pottery was made with stacked rings of earthen clay, smoothed, and fired in a simple oven, probably dug into the earth underneath a bonfire. Kilns weren't built until about 6000 B.C. (Sennebogen, 2009).
7. **A. Alcohol.** Some paleolithic cave art seems to depict shamans using alcohol to reach an altered state of consciousness. Pottery made purposeful fermentation simpler, leading to the development of wine (Hirst, 2011).
8. **B. Smelting.** Copper was probably the first smelted metal, then tin, lead, and silver. To heat the ore, charcoal—wood treated with fire—was the original fuel. Until the discovery of coal, it was the most efficient way to heat anything up (Editors of Encyclopaedia Britannica, 2019e).

Questions

9. Scholars now believe this integral communication technology was invented independently in four different parts of the globe.
    a. Writing
    b. Music
    c. Morse Code
    d. Rhetoric
10. This integral invention, often held up as a model of human ingenuity, was a relative latecomer in 3500 B.C.—probably because it doesn't exist in nature to inspire humans.
    a. The boat
    b. The wheel
    c. Shoes
    d. The flute
11. The largest leap forward in prehistoric agricultural technology was the invention of this tool, which is still evolving to this day.
    a. Shovel
    b. Hoe
    c. Drill
    d. Plow
12. This oldest type of surgery was practiced as early as 6000 B.C. based on the evidence of stone age skulls from Ukraine, Portugal, and North Africa.
    a. Cataract surgery
    b. Trepanation
    c. Heart surgery
    d. Appendectomy
13. This beautiful invention was made from crushed quartz pebbles in the late bronze age (1600–1200 B.C.), not from sand as it is today.
    a. Porcelain
    b. Concrete
    c. Glass
    d. Brick
14. This building material, used in Ancient Rome to build the Colosseum and the Parthenon, among other civic buildings, was only rediscovered in the 18th and 19th centuries.
    a. Concrete
    b. Limestone
    c. Granite
    d. Rebar
15. This piece of machinery, one of the earliest, uses lever technology to control the speed at which its toothed wheel turns around an axel.
    a. Pulley
    b. Weight
    c. Screw
    d. Gear
16. This clever invention harnesses the power of water and changes it into mechanical power, at first for the purposes of grinding grain or processing fiber.
    a. Water wheel
    b. Fiber optic cable
    c. Spinning wheel
    d. Sewing machine

Answers

9. **A. Writing.** The earliest writing we know of comes from Mesopotamia around 3200 B.C. It arose in Egypt around the same time. Without influence from these two cultures, Chinese writing appears around 1200 B.C., and writing in Guatemala and Mexico appears in 500 B.C. (Vasiloudis, 2022).
10. **B. The wheel.** Originally used to make the lives of potters easier, it took 300 years for someone to put them on a wagon after their invention in Mesopotamia. It may be one of the most taken-for-granted human inventions of all time, though its importance occasionally comes up when someone says they're "not trying to reinvent the wheel" as a form of modesty (Gambino, 2009).
11. **D. Plow.** Invented 10-13 million years ago in Mesopotamia's fertile crescent and other ancient breadbaskets like the Indus, Yangtze, and Nile valleys, the plow signified a radical shift from hunter-gatherer based societies to agricultural ones. It's undergone many transformations since the first hand plow, from ones driven by ox or horse power to the giant tractors of the modern age (Lal et al., 2007).
12. **B. Trepanation.** Drilling or otherwise making a hole in a person's head was considered a way to treat varied conditions in many cultures, including headaches, traumatic wounds, and epilepsy. The practice has been found in societies from all over the world, totally unrelated to one another, as far back as the paleolithic era (Cohut, 2019).
13. **C. Glass.** Though glass beads have been found from earlier periods, glass became all the rage in Egypt, Mesopotamia, and the Near East at this time. It was used for decorative purposes but also incorporated into structures as we do today—it was not transparent, however (Wilke, 2021).
14. **A. Concrete.** Modern concrete was invented by John Smeaton in 1956 and Joseph Aspdin invented Portland Cement in 1824. Today, most buildings are built with reinforced concrete, which has steel rebar throughout it (Bellis, 2019).
15. **D. Gear.** Gears were used throughout history for any number of inventions, especially those meant to measure—be it the orbits of the planets or the passage of time. Even today, gears are integral to modern machinery and innovation (Langston, 2022).
16. **A. Water wheel.** The horizontal water wheel relies on the forward action of flowing water from an aqueduct to turn the wheel. The overshot vertical water wheel relies on the gravity of water released above the wheel to turn it. The undershot vertical water wheel relies on a stream or river's natural current to turn it (Bellis, 2019b).

Questions

17. This early printing method developed in China; the first extant example of a book printed with it is a copy of the *Diamond Sutra* from the year 868.
    a. Movable type
    b. Hydraulic
    c. Wood block
    d. Daguerreotype
18. Before the modern version of this kind of bridge, it was made in China with twisted bamboo cables, such as the one built at Anlan in the year 300.
    a. Arch bridge
    b. Cantilever bridge
    c. Truss bridge
    d. Suspension bridge
19. The modern ratio for this 9th century discovery is 10:15:75, sulfur:charcoal:saltpeter.
    a. Sewer gas
    b. Gunpowder
    c. Matches
    d. Ammonia
20. The first mechanical clock was this kind of clock, invented during the late medieval or early renaissance period, replacing the water clock.
    a. Pendulum
    b. Digital
    c. Grandfather
    d. Cuckoo
21. Buttons were used as ornaments as early as the Indus Valley civilization. They started to serve a functional purpose as clothes became more close-fitting in…
    a. Republican Rome
    b. The European Middle Ages
    c. Chola Tamil Nadu
    d. Edo Japan
22. R. Tradwell received the first patent for this mechanical invention in Great Britain, 1763, based on science pioneered by Robert Hooke almost 100 years before.
    a. The escapement
    b. The bell rope
    c. The coil spring
    d. The sewing needle
23. This new form of media appeared in 1609, not long after Gutenberg's printing press gained favor in Europe.
    a. Radio
    b. Newspaper
    c. Novel
    d. Sheet music
24. Hans Lippershey, a Dutch lensmaker, usually gets credit for inventing this visual technology in 1608.
    a. Bifocals
    b. Camera
    c. Telescope
    d. Clockface

Answers

17. **C. Wood block.** Printing with wood blocks involves carving the wood, then rolling pigment onto the carving and hand-pressing it into the paper, vellum, or material. This development allowed many of the same design to be printed in a relatively short time (Bellis, 2019a).
18. **D. Suspension bridge.** Modern suspension bridge cables are made of thin steel wire twisted together. They're light and flexible, and therefore sway in a stiff wind, so larger ones need extra stabilizing (NOVA, 2000).
19. **B. Gunpowder.** The use of gunpowder in war spread from China to the Middle East via the Mongol Empire's quest for more land, and then to Europe via the Crusades (Brown University, 2009).
20. **A. Pendulum.** The pendulum, moving at a steady rate back and forth, was the heartbeat of the clock, regulating how fast or slow the escapement mechanism moved (Andrewes, 2006).
21. **B. European Middle Ages.** Though functional, buttons were also still ornamental, so much so that they were regulated by sumptuary laws. These laws regulated just how fancy someone could dress in a given city or state, down to the type of fur and how much, and even the colors different classes were allowed to wear. This allowed for the distinction of rank on sight, regardless of how much money a merchant or other non-noble had (Stewart, 2012).
22. **C. The coil spring.** Before Tradwell's invention, the leaf spring was used on carriages, which made for a much bumpier, louder ride than the new coil spring (Bellis, 2019c).
23. **B. Newspaper.** The earliest newspapers didn't list the city where they were printed, lest they be shut down by angry governments who wanted to control the news their people heard. Johann Carolus's *Relations: Aller Furnemmen* and Lucas Schulte's *Aviso Relations over Zeitung* are usually credited as the first (University of Minnesota, 2016).
24. **C. Telescope.** Two other Dutch inventors seem to have invented it simultaneously, one of whom, Zacharias Jansen, lived in the same town as Lippershey and was his main competitor. Lippershey was said to have been inspired by seeing two local children playing with discarded lenses to make things appear closer or bigger (Cox, 2017).

Questions

25. The first steam pump was developed in England by Thomas Savery in 1698 to do this.
    a. Lower miners into the shaft
    b. Pump water out of mines
    c. Speed up mining with explosives
    d. Shore up mine shaft supports
26. This modern invention made ice houses obsolete.
    a. Hair dryer
    b. Refrigerator
    c. Ice maker
    d. Convection oven
27. Before Richard Salter invented the spring scale in 1770, weighing something with scales always required a…
    a. Counterweight
    b. Anvil
    c. Pulley
    d. Gear
28. Joseph-Michel and Jacques-Étienne Montgolfier conducted the first successful experiments with this flight technology in 1783.
    a. Glider
    b. Prop plane
    c. Hot air balloon
    d. Zeppelin
29. This system of weights and measures was developed at the behest of the French Revolutionary government in 1789, who wanted a rational, standardized, and interrelated system.
    a. The British Standard system
    b. The Apothecary system
    c. The Metric system
    d. The Avoirdupois system
30. Scottish inventor Andrew Meikle revolutionized modern agriculture in 1788 with his invention of the…
    a. Lawnmower
    b. Threshing machine
    c. Millstone
    d. Aqueduct
31. In the 19th century, European tailors, inventors, and entrepreneurs made a rush at inventing a practical version of this machine to capitalize on the booming garment industry.
    a. Sewing machine
    b. Seam-ripper
    c. Hatpin
    d. Automatic measurement-taker
32. In this kind of engine, first made successfully in 1860, the fuel is ignited and burned inside the engine itself.
    a. Steam engine
    b. Gas turbine
    c. Internal combustion engine
    d. Electric engine

Answers

25. **B. Pump water out of mines.** Savery's design tended to explode due to built up steam pressure, but later designs by Newcomen and Watt got around the problem by using atmospheric pressure instead (Lira, 2001).
26. **B. Refrigerator.** Before the modern vapor-action refrigerator, and especially the discovery of Freon, which made it safe for homes, people purchased large blocks of ice from the arctic or kept snow and ice from winter in an ice house to cool provisions (Bellis, 2016a).
27. **A. Counterweight.** The spring scale works via gravity, which displaces the scale an amount that can be measured to determine force and then weight. This makes for a much less cumbersome weighing apparatus (P.T. Limited, 2017).
28. **C. Hot air balloon.** Their experiments caused such a stir that they were invited to Versailles to demonstrate before King Louis XVI and Queen Marie Antoinette. A rooster, a sheep, and a duck went up in the basket and returned to earth safely after an 8 minute flight (Sharp, 2019).
29. **C. The Metric system.** Although it was a time of deep turmoil for France, they commissioned the Paris Academy of Sciences, later re-Christened the Institute of France, to create a rational system for the nation. After some tweaks and improvements, it's the system most widely used throughout the world today (Smithsonian Institute, n.d.-b).
30. **B. Threshing machine.** Mielkle worked in a mill his whole life, so had ample opportunity to observe what made the process of hand-threshing so inefficient (Editors of Encyclopaedia Britannica, 2023a).
31. **A. Sewing machine.** Some of them, like Barthélemy Thimonnier in 1830, experienced dangerous pushback from their fellow tailors, who were afraid the new machine would steal their livelihoods.
32. **C. Internal combustion engine.** Most ICEs today are either a spark ignition engine, as in most domestic automobiles, or the compression ignition diesel engine (Office of Energy Efficiency & Renewable Energy, 2013).

Questions

33. Although he never got to build one, this engineer designed the first number-crunching computers in the 1820s and '30s.
    a. Steve Jobs
    b. Charles Babbage
    c. Bill Gates
    d. Thomas Edison
34. Before the incandescent electric light bulb Edison patented in 1879 and 80, these lamps demonstrated the potential of constant, electric light.
    a. Arc lamps
    b. Oil lamps
    c. Lava lamps
    d. Gas lamps
35. This necessary process of hardening rubber has been attributed to Charles Goodyear in Springfield, Massachusetts, in 1841.
    a. Smelting
    b. Vulcanizing
    c. Tamping
    d. Cementing
36. In 1907, chemist Leo Baekeland beat his rival, James Swinburne, to the office by just one day when he applied for the patent on…
    a. Portland cement
    b. The ten-speed bicycle
    c. Chewing gum
    d. Synthetic plastic
37. This process of heating liquids briefly to kill off harmful microorganisms is named for this French scientist.
    a. Marie Curie
    b. Louis Pasteur
    c. Paul Langevin
    d. Henry Dupont
38. Alexander Graham Bell found himself in a 20-year legal battle with these other claimants to the invention of the telephone.
    a. Gray and Meucci
    b. Watson and Crick
    c. Lewis and Clark
    d. Seals and Crofts
39. As a by-product of his work on the telegraph and telephone, this famous inventor came up with the first recording and playback device of its kind, the phonograph.
    a. Samuel Morse
    b. Henry Ford
    c. Thomas Edison
    d. Nikola Tesla
40. Due to the dangers that came with riding the Ordinary bicycle (think one large wheel in front, one small one in back), this redesign presented a safe, convenient, and inexpensive alternative for cheap individual transportation.
    a. The safety bicycle
    b. The mountain bicycle
    c. The side-by-side bicycle
    d. The Velocipede

Answers

33. **B. Charles Babbage.** He designed a few different "engines," the *Difference Engine No. 1* as the first calculating machine; the *Analytical Engine*, which was programmable using punch cards; and the *Difference Engine No. 2*, which not only tabulated but also automatically typeset printing plates of its results (Computer History Museum, 2019).
34. **A. Arc lamps.** These lamps are still used when intense brightness is required, like search lights or flood lights. They work via a spark of light caught between two carbon rods (Editors of Encyclopaedia Britannica, 2019).
35. **B. Vulcanizing.** In its natural form, rubber doesn't hold its shape well. Vulcanization is a process of introducing additives and heat to cure it, effectively (ScienceDirect, 2014).
36. **D. Synthetic plastic.** These were usually made with waste products from processing crude oil and gas, at the time. Now, plastics don't so much make use of excess as they do create excess (Science Museum, 2019).
37. **B. Louis Pasteur.** Pasteurization also kills many of the microorganisms responsible for spoilage, which is why ultra-pasteurized milk is shelf stable for a long time (Editors of Encyclopaedia Britannica, 2019).
38. **A. Gray and Meucci.** Elisha Gray and Antonio Meucci both worked on a telephone, and took steps toward patenting their designs, but Bell got the patent first (Science Reference Section, Library of Congress, 2022).
39. **C. Thomas Edison.** The vibrations of the spoken word made an embossing needle indent paraffin paper in a specific way, recording the tones and sounds. This inspired Edison to try it with a metal cylinder and foil, which worked beautifully (Library of Congress, 2015a).
40. **A. The safety bicycle.** With its equal-sized wheels, chain drive, and gears for different uses, the safety bicycle was the first real modern bike. The addition of the pneumatic tire, invented by John Boyd Dunlop, made it even better (Smithsonian Institute, n.d.-c).

Questions

41. Multiple inventors deserve the credit for making television technology possible, including this German inventor of the cathode ray tube.
    a. Robert Bunsen
    b. Karl Braun
    c. Nikola Tesla
    d. Melitta Bentz
42. In 1928, Dr. Alexander Fleming made this accidental discovery by leaving a petri dish of bacteria out while he was away on holiday.
    a. Arsenic
    b. DNA
    c. Penicillin
    d. Tuberculosis
43. In 1944, Otto Hahn won the Nobel Prize for Chemistry for discovering this process, which had almost unlimited energy potential. But the woman who explained the process, Lise Meitner, never got credit.
    a. Nuclear fission
    b. Searing
    c. Pressurizing
    d. Vulcanizing
44. This analog computer, a kind of proto-videogame, engaged visitors at the 1950 Canadian National Exposition in Tic-Tac-Toe.
    a. Helen the Heavy
    b. Bertie the Brain
    c. Alexander the Great
    d. Tila the Ticker
45. Reynold B. Johnson, an IBM engineer, came up with this essential data storage element in 1954.
    a. USB port
    b. RAM
    c. Heat sink
    d. Hard disk drive
46. The launch of the first Space Shuttle, Columbia, in 1981 was different from every space flight that had come before it because…
    a. The shuttle was reusable
    b. They weren't going to the moon
    c. They had to stop for gas
    d. There were no astronauts aboard
47. The first commercially produced cell phone, the Motorola Dynatac 800X, was also known as…
    a. The One
    b. The Brick
    c. The Worst
    d. The Wolf
48. While working at CERN in 1989, Tim Berners-Lee wrote up a proposal to combine data tech, new computers, and hypertext into…
    a. NFTs
    b. The World Wide Web
    c. Blogging
    d. Social Media

Answers

41. **B. Karl Braun.** The cathode ray tube (CRT) became the basis for the glass display of the CRT television, invented by Philo Farnsworth in 1927. Nowadays, most TVS are flat-screen liquid crystal displays or LCD, but the CRT is where it all started (Pruitt, 2021).
42. **C. Penicillin.** Mold was growing on the dish, which seemed to be inhibiting the growth of the bacteria. It wasn't until 1941 when another group of chemists figured out how to purify the penicillin from the mold, albeit at an achingly slow rate until after WWII (Science Museum, 2021).
43. **A. Nuclear fission.** Lise Meitner had to leave her laboratory in Berlin once the Nazis made life too dangerous for Jewish Germans, but she kept in contact with her partner, Otto Frisch, and Hahn via telephone and occasional visits from them (Tretkoff, 2019).
44. **B. Bertie the Brain.** Bertie was the closest to a video game, but he wasn't the first mechanized game-playing invention, though. The Nimatron was an electric-powered machine that played all comers at Nim in 1940. The Magnavox was the first home-gaming system in the same vein of the Playstation and XBox consoles of today (Dyson, 2020).
45. **D. Hard disk drive.** The first external HDD, the Model 350, had 50 24-inch diameter disks stacked one on top of the other and measured 5 feet tall and 6 feet wide. It couldn't be bought, only rented for $750 a month (Computer History Museum, n.d.).
46. **A. The shuttle was reusable.** Before Columbia, the STS-1, space flight meant a crew capsule was attached to a rocket and shot into space. The crew capsule came back to earth but couldn't be reused (NASA, 2007).
47. **B. The Brick.** This huge phone looked, unsurprisingly, like a brick being held to the caller's ear. It cost upwards of $5000 at the time (Ali, 2018).
48. **B. The World Wide Web.** The very first website is still located at http://info.cern.ch/hypertext/WWW/TheProject.html, and it describes hypertext, the people involved in the WWW project, and what would now be considered old-timey browser help among other topics (CERN, 2019).

Questions

49. This data storage technology began in 1991 as a way to decentralize records so they couldn't be tampered with or misdated.
    a. RAM
    b. The cloud
    c. Blockchain
    d. Flash memory
50. This large language model chatbot, introduced in 2022, started a fervent discussion about AI and the future of creative professions.
    a. YouTube
    b. TikTok
    c. WhatsApp
    d. ChatGPT

Answers

49. **C. Blockchain.** Now a major pillar of the cryptocurrency movement, blockchain technology stores data in chunks in multiple places, so no one person can change a record without changing them in *all* the places it's stored. At the moment, it still has some kinks to work out, as it's a highly energy-inefficient process (Rodeck, 2021).
50. **D. ChatGPT.** While the large language model produces interesting and occasionally helpful results, it's notorious for not "thinking" the way humans do when we converse and for not fact-checking itself. For now (Sundar, 2023).

Conclusion

I hope that was as fun for you as it was for me, and I hope your metaphorical debate quiver is full of arrows straight out of history, now. It's been an adventure, over the length and breadth of the world, of human accomplishment and folly, of artistic and mathematical and mechanical inspiration. Hopefully, you found a rabbit hole or two to jump down on your own. A deep dive off any one of these 500 questions can lead to wild, wonderful, sometimes weird worlds, and every single one of them is worth it.

For me, history has always provided a treasure trove of questions, answers, and questions that are answered with more questions. As much as that third thing might sound frustrating, I find it's the food that feeds an active, curious mind. It satisfies it *and* makes it interested in learning more, going deeper, and maybe even going where others haven't before.

As much as history feels like a static thing from the viewpoint of the present, our understanding of it is constantly changing. DNA technology, new discoveries in archaeology, long-lost books being found, biased interpretations being overturned and righted. These things happen every day, and aren't just the province of professional academics. An interested amateur can make world-changing discoveries. Take Phillipa Langley, MBE, the amateur historian and Richard III enthusiast responsible for finding the lost burial site of the last Plantagenet king of England himself… under a parking lot in Leicester in 2012. Sure, we won't all get to dig up maligned historical figures in the middle of big cities—but that's just one example of what can happen when history comes alive in a curious mind. It's Indiana Jones but *real*, tangible, if just as strange and wonderful. Stories we thought we knew take on a new shape, and the world becomes a little bigger and a little brighter for everyone.

We began this journey with a quote from Winston Churchill, an avid historian as well as international political figure. Let's end it with one, too:

Those who fail to learn from history are condemned to repeat it.

–Winston Churchill, 1948

If you enjoyed our tour of history, please drop by and give the book a review—and don't forget to share it with your friends! Trivia is always a "the more, the merrier" situation, after all.

Message from the Author

Dear Friends,

Thanks for reading my history book!

I was always the biggest History Geek growing up. By grade 7 I had memorized all the names of the Greek Gods in mythology and could also tell you why Hitler failed in his quest for world domination during WW2. You know that nerd at the back that always raised his hands to answer the teacher's questions? - That was me during Social Studies class.

I wrote this book to spark the love of history for everyone. Learning about history is like eating a nutritious apple – it should be taken daily when you're young so that you reap the health benefits as you age. It's helped me tremendously in my personal relationships & career and it's my hope that it will help yours too.

Your reviews are important to me and I will read each one personally. It will also help others discover this book as you did. Thanks for your support!

http://www.amazon.com/review/create-review?&asin=B0CLT77DXK

Kind Regards,

Bryan Mack - Curious Publications

References

Accademia. (2019). *Michelangelo's David: Admire world's greatest sculpture at Accademia Gallery*. Accademia.org. https://www.accademia.org/explore-museum/artworks/michelangelos-david/

AICTE. (n.d.). *Ancient universities in India*. https://www.aicte-india.org/downloads/ancient.pdf

Al-Sharif, H. (2019, January 30). *Symbolism in the Arnolfini Portrait*. Artmejo. https://artmejo.com/symbolism-in-the-arnolfini-portrait/

Alex, B. (2019, March 31). *The great Aztec temple*. Discover Magazine. https://www.discovermagazine.com/the-sciences/the-great-aztec-temple

Ali, R. (2018, April 6). *History of mobile phones | What was the first mobile phone?* USwitch Mobile Phone Deals; uSwitch. https://www.uswitch.com/mobiles/guides/history-of-mobile-phones/

Ambury, J. M. (2022). *Socrates*. Internet Encyclopedia of Philosophy. https://iep.utm.edu/socrates/

American Experience. (n.d.). *Race and the Army during World War II | American Experience | PBS*. Www.pbs.org. https://www.pbs.org/wgbh/americanexperience/features/alaska-WWII/

Amsen, E. (2019, May 2). *Leonardo da Vinci's scientific studies, 500 years later*. Forbes. https://www.forbes.com/sites/evaamsen/2019/05/02/leonardo-da-vincis-scientific-studies-500-years-later/?sh=1df819fc7f46

Andrew, C. (n.d.). *The establishment of the Secret Service Bureau | MI5 - the Security Service*. Www.mi5.Gov.uk. https://www.mi5.gov.uk/the-establishment-of-the-secret-service-bureau

Andrewes, W. J. H. (2006). A chronicle of timekeeping. *Scientific American Sp*, *16*(1), 46–55. https://doi.org/10.1038/scientificamerican0206-46sp

Andrews, E. (2018, August 29). *11 Things you may not know about Ancient Egypt*. History. https://www.history.com/news/11-things-you-may-not-know-about-ancient-egypt

Applied History Research Group . (1998). *End of Europe's Middle Ages - Holy Roman Empire*. Umb.edu; University of Calgary. https://www.faculty.umb.edu/gary_zabel/Courses/Phil%20281b/Philosophy%20of%20Magic/Dante.%20etc/Philosophers/End/holy.html

Armstrong, D. (2021, September 11). *The Ciompi Revolt: Florence after the Black Death*. Wondrium Daily. https://www.wondriumdaily.com/the-ciompi-revolt-florence-after-the-black-death/

Asante, M. K. (2007, August 21). *The ideological origins of chattel slavery in the British world*. National Museums Liverpool. https://www.liverpoolmuseums.org.uk/ideological-origins-of-chattel-slavery-british-world

Asia for Educators. (n.d.). The Constitution of Prince Shotuku. In *Asia for Educators*. Columbia University. http://afe.easia.columbia.edu/ps/japan/shotoku.pdf

Atlas Obscura. (2017, May 9). *Nilometer: This ancient instrument measured the waters of the Nile*. Atlas Obscura. https://www.atlasobscura.com/places/nilometer

Augustyn, A. (2018). Nelson Mandela. In *Encyclopedia Britannica*. https://www.britannica.com/biography/Nelson-Mandela

Bayeux Museum. (n.d.). *The Battle of Hastings*. Bayeux Museum. https://www.bayeuxmuseum.com/en/the-bayeux-tapestry/discover-the-bayeux-tapestry/the_battle_of_hastings/

BBC. (2014a). *BBC - history - Mao Zedong*. Www.bbc.co.uk. https://www.bbc.co.uk/history/historic_figures/mao_zedong.shtml

BBC. (2014b). *Historic figures: Ayatollah Khomeini (1900-1989)*. Bbc.co.uk. https://www.bbc.co.uk/history/historic_figures/khomeini_ayatollah.shtml

BBC. (2014c). *Historic figures: Maximilien Robespierre (1758-1794)*. Www.bbc.co.uk. https://www.bbc.co.uk/history/historic_figures/robespierre_maximilien.shtml

BBC History. (2014). *BBC - history - Erasmus*. Bbc.co.uk. https://www.bbc.co.uk/history/historic_figures/erasmus.shtml

Bellis, M. (2011). *History of the spinning wheel*. ThoughtCo. https://www.thoughtco.com/spinning-wheel-evolution-1992414

Bellis, M. (2016a). *The history of the refrigerator.* ThoughtCo. https://www.thoughtco.com/history-of-refrigerator-and-freezers-4072564

Bellis, M. (2016b, August 23). *The history of the water wheel.* ThoughtCo; ThoughtCo. https://www.thoughtco.com/history-of-waterwheel-4077881

Bellis, M. (2019a). *Read the detailed timeline of printing and printing processes.* ThoughtCo. https://www.thoughtco.com/history-of-printing-and-printing-processes-1992329

Bellis, M. (2019b). *The history of concrete and cement.* ThoughtCo. https://www.thoughtco.com/history-of-concrete-and-cement-1991653

Bellis, M. (2019c, August 19). *What is Hooke's law?* ThoughtCo. https://www.thoughtco.com/spring-coils-physics-and-workings-4075522

Beyer, G. (2022, June 10). *Utterly impregnable: Castles in Europe & how they were built to last.* TheCollector. https://www.thecollector.com/castles-in-europe-how-were-they-built/

Beyer, G. (2023a, March 1). *Vasco da Gama: Explorer & adventurer.* TheCollector. https://www.thecollector.com/vasco-da-gama-explorer-adventurer/

Beyer, G. (2023b, March 15). *The Significance of Alfred the Great.* TheCollector. https://www.thecollector.com/who-was-alfred-the-great/

Bileta, V. (2021, October 19). *Agrippina the Younger: Rome's first true empress.* TheCollector. https://www.thecollector.com/agrippina-the-younger/

Biography.com. (2021, June 23). *Amerigo Vespucci - Ship, route & timeline.* Biography. https://www.biography.com/history-culture/amerigo-vespucci

Biography.com Editors. (2014, September 9). *Saint Thomas Aquinas.* Biography. https://www.biography.com/religious-figure/saint-thomas-aquinas

Biography.com Editors. (2021, April 20). *Lucrezia Borgia.* Biography. https://www.biography.com/crime/lucrezia-borgia

Biondich, A. S., & Joslin, J. D. (2016). Coca: The history and medical significance of an ancient Andean tradition. *Emergency Medicine International, 2016*, 1–5. https://doi.org/10.1155/2016/4048764

Björklund, J., Seftigen, K., Stoffel, M., Fonti, M. V., Kottlow, S., Frank, D. C., Esper, J., Fonti, P., Goosse, H., Grudd, H., Gunnarson, B. E., Nievergelt, D., Pellizzari, E., Carrer, M., & von Arx, G. (2023). Fennoscandian tree-ring anatomy shows a warmer modern than medieval climate. *Nature, 620*(7972), 97–103. https://doi.org/10.1038/s41586-023-06176-4

Bloom, I. (2009). *Introduction to Daoism | Asia for educators | Columbia university.* Columbia.edu. http://afe.easia.columbia.edu/special/china_1000bce_daoism.htm

Boissoneault, L. (2017, November 9). *Was Vichy France a puppet government or a willing Nazi collaborator?* Smithsonian; Smithsonian.com. https://www.smithsonianmag.com/history/vichy-government-france-world-war-ii-willingly-collaborated-nazis-180967160/

Bomboy, S. (2021). *The vote that led to the 19th Amendment - National Constitution Center.* National Constitution Center – Constitutioncenter.org. https://constitutioncenter.org/blog/the-man-and-his-mom-who-gave-women-the-vote

Borowski, S. (2012, December 17). *Myths of the Mayan Long Count calendar | American Association for the Advancement of Science.* Www.aaas.org. https://www.aaas.org/myths-mayan-long-count-calendar

Brain, J. (2020, April 20). *The Scientific Revolution.* Historic UK. https://www.historic-uk.com/HistoryUK/HistoryofBritain/The-Scientific-Revolution/

Briney, A. (2020, January 23). *Discover the Age of Exploration.* ThoughtCo. https://www.thoughtco.com/age-of-exploration-1435006

British Museum. (2016). *Chinese jade: an introduction.* Khan Academy. https://www.khanacademy.org/humanities/art-asia/imperial-china/neolithic-art-china/a/chinese-jade-an-introduction

Brooks, S. (2019). *The Byzantine State under Justinian I (Justinian the Great).* Metmuseum.org. https://www.metmuseum.org/toah/hd/just/hd_just.htm

Brown University. (2009). *Gunpowder: Origins in the East.* Brown.edu. https://www.brown.edu/Departments/Joukowsky_Institute/courses/13things/7687.html

Bruhns, C. (2017, March 27). *Legacy of Petrarch - tensions in Renaissance cities - The University of Chicago library.* Www.lib.uchicago.edu. https://www.lib.uchicago.edu/collex/exhibits/tensions-renaissance-cities/double-rivalry-rome-and-florence/legacy-petrarch/

Bryant, C. (2020, August 27). *1565: The massacre of the Huguenots by the Spanish in Florida.* Who Is Jean Ribault? French Huguenots in Florida. https://jeanribault.org/1565-the-massacre-of-the-huguenots-by-the-spanish-in-florida/

Burdrovich, N. (2020, February 5). *Everyone was drinking! Inside an ancient three-day festival of wine.* Www.getty.edu. https://www.getty.edu/news/everyone-was-drinking-inside-an-ancient-3-day-festival-of-wine/

Burgess, A. (2023, April 5). *Exploring Medieval chivalric romance.* ThoughtCo. https://www.thoughtco.com/the-medieval-chivalric-romance-740720

Canadian Museum of History. (n.d.). *Jean Nicollet 1634 | Virtual Museum of New France.* Canadian Museum of History. https://www.historymuseum.ca/virtual-museum-of-new-france/the-explorers/jean-nicollet-1634/

Carr, S. M. (n.d.). *The Four Elements.* Www.mun.ca. https://www.mun.ca/biology/scarr/4270_The_Four_Elements.html

Cartledge, P. (2020, November 20). *Nine things you really ought to know about the ancient city of Thebes.* Www.panmacmillan.com. https://www.panmacmillan.com/blogs/history/paul-cartlege-ancient-thebes-facts

Cartwright, M. (2018, November 22). *Feudalism.* World History Encyclopedia. https://www.worldhistory.org/Feudalism/

Castelow, E. (2017). *World War One and the triggers for war.* Historic UK. https://www.historic-uk.com/HistoryUK/HistoryofBritain/The-Causes-of-World-War-One/

Cavallo, A. S. (1993). *Medieval tapestries in the Metropolitan Museum of Art.* Metropolitan Museum Of Art.

CERN. (2019, September 23). *A short history of the Web | CERN.* Home.cern; CERN. https://home.cern/science/computing/birth-web/short-history-web

Cervera, O. C. (2022, July 27). *The Aluxes of yesterday and today - Yucatan Today.* Yucatantoday.com. https://yucatantoday.com/en/the-aluxes-of-yesterday-and-today/

Chang, K. (2008, February 29). The grim story of Maya blue. *The New York Times.* https://www.nytimes.com/2008/02/29/science/29bluew.html

Ciotola, L. (2013). *Crusader disaster at Nicopolis.* Warfare History Network. https://warfarehistorynetwork.com/article/crusader-disaster-at-nicopolis/

Citino, R. (2021, November 11). *Pearl Harbor attack, December 7, 1941.* The National WWII Museum | New Orleans. https://www.nationalww2museum.org/war/topics/pearl-harbor-december-7-1941

CNN. (2019). *Tobacco under attack.* Cnn.com. http://edition.cnn.com/US/9705/tobacco/history/

Cochran, L. (n.d.). *The 1619 landing — Virginia's first Africans report & FAQs* . Hampton.gov. https://hampton.gov/3580/The-1619-Landing-Report-FAQs

Cohen, R. (2002, April 4). *The history of horseshoes.* Dressage Today. https://dressagetoday.com/horse-health/history-of-horseshoes/

Cohut, M. (2019, September 6). *Trepanation: Our ancestors' idea of neurosurgery.* Www.medicalnewstoday.com. https://www.medicalnewstoday.com/articles/326281

Coman, S. (n.d.). *Asuka period, an introduction (article).* Khan Academy. https://www.khanacademy.org/humanities/art-asia/art-japan/x97ec695a:asuka-period/a/asuka-period-an-introduction

Computer History Museum. (n.d.). *1956: First commercial hard disk drive shipped | The Storage Engine | Computer History Museum.* Www.computerhistory.org. https://www.computerhistory.org/storageengine/first-commercial-hard-disk-drive-shipped/

Computer History Museum. (2019). *The engines | Babbage Engine | Computer History Museum.* Computerhistory.org. https://www.computerhistory.org/babbage/engines/

Cordell, D. D. (2019). Patrice Lumumba | biography, facts, & death. In *Encyclopædia Britannica.* https://www.britannica.com/biography/Patrice-Lumumba

Cox, L. (2017, December 21). *Who invented the telescope?* Space.com. https://www.space.com/21950-who-invented-the-telescope.html

Cuffia, A. (n.d.). *Winchester rifle: A resource guide: Introduction.* Guides.loc.gov. https://guides.loc.gov/winchester-rifle

Curry, A. (2022). Meeting the ancestors: History of Ashkenazi Jews revealed in medieval DNA. *AAAS Articles DO Group.* https://doi.org/10.1126/science.adg0492

Daniels, R. (2023, September 17). *Leon Trotsky - role in Soviet government.* Encyclopedia Britannica. https://www.britannica.com/biography/Leon-Trotsky/Role-in-Soviet-government

Daniyal, S. (2015, June 30). *Fact check: India wasn't the first place Sanskrit was recorded – it was Syria.* Scroll.in. https://scroll.in/article/737715/fact-check-india-wasnt-the-first-place-sanskrit-was-recorded-it-was-syria

Dash, M. (2012, August 10). *The demonization of Empress Wu.* Smithsonian. https://www.smithsonianmag.com/history/the-demonization-of-empress-wu-20743091/

davide. (2019, April 10). *Madeira discovery and settlement.* Portuguese Historical Museum. https://portuguesemuseum.org/?page_id=1808&category=&exhibit=24&event=176

Dawsey, J. (2021, November 17). *Nazi Germany, Imperial Japan, and the Anti-Comintern Pact.* The National WWII Museum | New Orleans. https://www.nationalww2museum.org/war/articles/nazi-germany-imperial-japan-anti-comintern-pact

de Ferdinandy, M. (2019). Charles V. In *Encyclopædia Britannica.* https://www.britannica.com/biography/Charles-V-Holy-Roman-emperor

Department of Asian Art. (2019a). *Jōmon culture (ca. 10,500–ca. 300 B.C.).* Metmuseum.org. https://www.metmuseum.org/toah/hd/jomo/hd_jomo.htm

Department of Asian Art. (2019b). *Yayoi culture (ca. 300 B.C.–300 A.D.).* Metmuseum.org. https://www.metmuseum.org/toah/hd/yayo/hd_yayo.htm

DiGrado, E. (2005). *Virgin vestals.* Departments.kings.edu. https://departments.kings.edu/womens_history/vestals.html

Discover Peru.org. (2019). *The Inca and his family | Discover Peru.* Discover-Peru.org. http://www.discover-peru.org/inca-family/

Dodds, J. D. (1992). *al-Andalus : the art of Islamic Spain.* Metropolitan Museum Of Art.

Donnelley, A. (2002). *Ani Pachen Dolma (1933-2002).* Tricycle: The Buddhist Review. https://tricycle.org/magazine/ani-pachen-dolma-1933-2002/

Duignan, B., & Cranston, M. (2018). Jean-Jacques Rousseau. In *Encyclopædia Britannica.* https://www.britannica.com/biography/Jean-Jacques-Rousseau

Dyson, J.-P. (2020, November 25). *What was the first video game?* The Strong National Museum of Play. https://www.museumofplay.org/blog/what-was-the-first-video-game/

Editors of Encyclopaedia Britannica. (1998a, July 20). *Portolan chart | Britannica.* Www.britannica.com. https://www.britannica.com/technology/portolan-chart

Editors of Encyclopaedia Britannica. (1998b, July 20). *Virginal | musical instrument.* Encyclopedia Britannica. https://www.britannica.com/art/virginal

Editors of Encyclopaedia Britannica. (2019a). Fulvia | wife of Mark Antony. In *Encyclopædia Britannica.* https://www.britannica.com/biography/Fulvia-wife-of-Mark-Antony

Editors of Encyclopaedia Britannica. (2019b). Léopold Senghor | president of Senegal. In *Encyclopædia Britannica.* https://www.britannica.com/biography/Leopold-Senghor

Editors of Encyclopaedia Britannica. (2019c). Michael Collins | biography & facts. In *Encyclopædia Britannica.* https://www.britannica.com/biography/Michael-Collins-Irish-statesman

Editors of Encyclopaedia Britannica. (2019d). Nicolaus Copernicus - Copernicus's astronomical work. In *Encyclopædia Britannica.* https://www.britannica.com/biography/Nicolaus-Copernicus/Copernicuss-astronomical-work

Editors of Encyclopaedia Britannica. (2019e). Smelting | Definition & facts. In *Encyclopædia Britannica.* https://www.britannica.com/technology/smelting

Editors of Encyclopaedia Britannica. (2021a, November 11). *Cape Bojador | Africa, history, & Point of No Return | Britannica.* Www.britannica.com. https://www.britannica.com/place/Cape-Bojador

Editors of Encyclopaedia Britannica. (2021b, November 14). *Carrack | ship.* Encyclopedia Britannica. https://www.britannica.com/technology/carrack

Editors of Encyclopaedia Britannica. (2023a, January 1). *Andrew Meikle | Scottish inventor.* Encyclopedia Britannica. https://www.britannica.com/biography/Andrew-Meikle

Editors of Encyclopaedia Britannica. (2023b, May 22). *Mehmed I | Ottoman sultan.* Encyclopedia Britannica. https://www.britannica.com/biography/Mehmed-I

Editors of Encyclopaedia Britannica. (2023c, May 28). *Étienne Brûlé | Canadian explorer.* Www.britannica.com. https://www.britannica.com/biography/Etienne-Brule

Editors of Encyclopaedia Britannica. (2023d, September 13). *Agostinho Neto | biography & facts.* Www.britannica.com. https://www.britannica.com/biography/Agostinho-Neto

Editors of Encyclopaedia Britannica . (2003, May 15). *Ho Chi Minh summary | Britannica.* Www.britannica.com. https://www.britannica.com/summary/Ho-Chi-Minh

Editors of Encyclopaedia Britannica . (2019). Pasteurization | heating process. In *Encyclopædia Britannica.* https://www.britannica.com/technology/pasteurization

Editors of Encyclopedia Britannica. (2015). Djoser | king of Egypt. In *Encyclopædia Britannica.* https://www.britannica.com/biography/Djoser

Editors of Encyclopedia Britannica. (2018a). Mary Wollstonecraft. In *Encyclopædia Britannica.* https://www.britannica.com/biography/Mary-Wollstonecraft

Editors of Encyclopedia Britannica. (2018b). Saint Teresa of Avila | Biography, facts, & works. In *Encyclopædia Britannica.* https://www.britannica.com/biography/Saint-Teresa-of-Avila

Editors of Encyclopedia Britannica. (2018c). Renaissance. In *Encyclopædia Britannica.* https://www.britannica.com/event/Renaissance

Editors of Encyclopedia Britannica. (2018d). Battle of the Bulge | summary & significance. In *Encyclopædia Britannica.* https://www.britannica.com/event/Battle-of-the-Bulge

Editors of Encyclopedia Britannica. (2019). Arc lamp. In *Encyclopædia Britannica.* https://www.britannica.com/technology/arc-lamp

Editors of Encyclopedia Britannica. (2019a). Emmeline Pankhurst | biography & facts. In *Encyclopædia Britannica.* https://www.britannica.com/biography/Emmeline-Pankhurst

Editors of Encyclopedia Britannica. (2019b). Spartacus | history, facts, & influence. In *Encyclopædia Britannica.* https://www.britannica.com/biography/Spartacus-Roman-gladiator

Editors of Encyclopedia Britannica. (2020). League of Nations. In *Encyclopædia Britannica.* https://www.britannica.com/topic/League-of-Nations

Editors of Encyclopedia Britannica. (2023, June 6). *Luís de Camões - poetry, epic, Lusiads | Britannica.* Www.britannica.com. https://www.britannica.com/biography/Luis-de-Camoes/Literary-works

Englert, W. (2019). *Greek theater.* Reed.edu. https://www.reed.edu/humanities/110tech/Theater.html

Falvey Library. (2019). *Library exhibits :: Dante's biography.* Villanova.edu. https://exhibits.library.villanova.edu/dante-illustrated/dante-s-biography

Forest, H. (2018, November 16). *The Kofun period (c.250–538 CE): An introduction to Japanese history.* Medium. https://hercynianforest.medium.com/the-kofun-period-c-250-538-ce-an-introduction-to-japanese-history-317e5e35b978

Gambino, M. (2009, June 17). *A salute to the wheel.* Smithsonian; Smithsonian.com. https://www.smithsonianmag.com/science-nature/a-salute-to-the-wheel-31805121/

Garthwaite, J. (2015, February 12). *What we know about the earliest history of chocolate.* Smithsonian Magazine. https://www.smithsonianmag.com/history/archaeology-chocolate-180954243/

Gasparotto, D. (2021, September 1). *Artemisia Gentileschi: The woman, the artist.* Www.getty.edu. https://www.getty.edu/news/artemisia-gentileschi-the-woman-the-artist/

Geller, L. (2018, October 21). *Folger Library – Churchill's Shakespeare.* The International Churchill Society. https://winstonchurchill.org/resources/in-the-media/churchill-in-the-news/folger-library-churchills-shakespeare/

Gilder Lehrman Institute of American History. (n.d.). *Lord Dunmore's Proclamation, 1775 | Gilder Lehrman Institute of American History.* Www.gilderlehrman.org. https://www.gilderlehrman.org/history-resources/spotlight-primary-source/lord-dunmores-proclamation-1775

Gill, N. S. (2019). *Biography of Tarquin the Proud, last Etruscan king of Rome*. ThoughtCo. https://www.thoughtco.com/tarquin-the-proud-119623

Gill, N. S. (2020, January 28). *Meet Nabopolassar, King of Babylon*. ThoughtCo. https://www.thoughtco.com/babylonian-king-nabopolassar-120004

Gill, V. (2010, August 26). Oldest evidence of arrows found. *BBC News.* https://www.bbc.com/news/science-environment-11086110

Giovinazzo, D. (2020, October 15). *Anita Garibaldi: The heroine of two worlds (author interview).* ITALY Magazine. https://www.italymagazine.com/featured-story/anita-garibaldi-heroine-two-worlds-author-interview

Good, A. (2021). *Knucklebones.* JHU Archaeological Museum. https://archaeologicalmuseum.jhu.edu/class-projects/archaeology-of-daily-life/childhood/knucklebones/

Goodrick-Clarke, N. (n.d.). *Paracelsus.* Web.stanford.edu. https://web.stanford.edu/class/history13/Readings/clarke.htm

Gordon, E. C. (1986). The fate of Sir Hugh Willoughby and his companions: A new conjecture. *The Geographical Journal, 152*(2), 243–247. https://doi.org/10.2307/634766

Gould, A. (2017, August 3). *Johannes Kepler: His life, his laws and times.* NASA. https://www.nasa.gov/kepler/education/johannes

Greek Legends and Myths. (2018). *Mount Olympus in Greek mythology.* Greek Legends and Myths. https://www.greeklegendsandmyths.com/mount-olympus.html

Greenspan, J. (2012, November 5). *Guy Fawkes Day: A brief history.* History. https://www.history.com/news/guy-fawkes-day-a-brief-history

Grescoe, T. (2021, November). *Culinary detectives try to recover the formula for a deliciously fishy Roman condiment*. Smithsonian Magazine. https://www.smithsonianmag.com/arts-culture/recoving-the-recipe-for-garum-180978846/

Gruber, S. (n.d.). *Rudolf I of Habsburg: From "poor count" to King of the Romans.* Die Welt Der Habsburger. https://www.habsburger.net/en/chapter/rudolf-i-habsburg-poor-count-king-romans

Guilmartin, J. F. (2023, September 12). *Military technology - Early use of artillery.* Encyclopedia Britannica. https://www.britannica.com/technology/military-technology/Early-use-of-artillery

Hammer, E. (2019). *Shinto.* Asia Society. https://asiasociety.org/education/shinto

Hand, J. O. (2018). *Artist info.* Nga.gov. https://www.nga.gov/collection/artist-info.1256.html

Hanna, W. A. (2018). Sukarno | president of Indonesia. In *Encyclopædia Britannica.* https://www.britannica.com/biography/Sukarno

Hansen, V. (2002). *Paper.* Smithsonian Folklife Festival. https://festival.si.edu/2002/the-silk-road/paper/smithsonian

Haskew, M. (2015, September 9). *Rollo the Viking, first ruler of Normandy.* Warfare History Network. https://warfarehistorynetwork.com/rollo-the-viking-first-ruler-of-normandy/

Hayward, N. (2018). *Susan B. Anthony.* National Women's History Museum; Nancy Hayward. https://www.womenshistory.org/education-resources/biographies/susan-b-anthony

Hershock, P. (2015). *Chan Buddhism (Stanford Encyclopedia of Philosophy).* Stanford.edu. https://plato.stanford.edu/entries/buddhism-chan/

Hickman, K. (2023, April 5). *World War II Europe: Fighting in North Africa, Sicily, and Italy.* ThoughtCo. https://www.thoughtco.com/world-war-ii-north-africa-italy-2361454

Hicks, S. (2013, November 13). *John Calvin's Geneva – Stephen Hicks, Ph.D.* Stephen Hicks, Ph.D. https://www.stephenhicks.org/2010/11/27/john-calvins-geneva/

Hill, J. (2021, May 9). Sophie Scholl: Student who resisted Hitler and inspires Germany. *BBC News.* https://www.bbc.com/news/world-europe-57008360

Hirst, K. K. (2011). *How long have humans been consuming alcohol?* ThoughtCo. https://www.thoughtco.com/history-of-alcohol-a-timeline-170889

Hirst, K. K. (2019). *Chinampas: Highly productive and ecologically sound ancient farms.* ThoughtCo. https://www.thoughtco.com/chinampa-floating-gardens-170337

History. com Editors. (2009, December 2). *Louisiana Purchase.* History; A&E Television Networks. https://www.history.com/topics/19th-century/louisiana-purchase

History.com Editors. (2009a, October 15). *Civil War.* History.com; A&E Television Networks. https://www.history.com/topics/american-civil-war/american-civil-war-history

History.com Editors. (2009b, October 27). *Aztecs.* History; A&E Television Networks. https://www.history.com/topics/ancient-americas/aztecs

History.com Editors. (2009c, October 27). *Boston Tea Party.* History; A&E Television Networks. https://www.history.com/topics/american-revolution/boston-tea-party

History.com Editors. (2009d, October 29). *Malcolm X.* History; A&E Television Networks. https://www.history.com/topics/black-history/malcolm-x

History.com Editors. (2009e, October 29). *New Deal.* History; A&E Television Networks. https://www.history.com/topics/great-depression/new-deal

History.com Editors. (2009f, October 29). *Operation Barbarossa.* History.com; A&E Television Networks. https://www.history.com/topics/world-war-ii/operation-barbarossa

History.com Editors. (2009g, October 29). *Punic Wars.* History. https://www.history.com/topics/ancient-rome/punic-wars

History.com Editors. (2009h, October 29). *Treaty of Versailles.* History; A&E Television Networks. https://www.history.com/topics/world-war-i/treaty-of-versailles-1

History.com Editors. (2009i, November 4). *Vikings.* History; A&E Television Networks. https://www.history.com/topics/exploration/vikings-history

History.com Editors. (2009j, November 5). *Warsaw falls to German forces.* History. https://www.history.com/this-day-in-history/poland-surrenders

History.com Editors. (2009k, November 9). *Christopher Columbus.* History.com; A&E Television Networks. https://www.history.com/topics/exploration/christopher-columbus

History.com Editors. (2009l, November 9). *Genghis Khan.* History. https://www.history.com/topics/asian-history/genghis-khan

History.com Editors. (2009m, November 9). *Mexican-American War.* HIstory; A&E Television Networks. https://www.history.com/topics/19th-century/mexican-american-war

History.com Editors. (2009n, November 9). *Morse code & the telegraph.* History; A&E Television Networks. https://www.history.com/topics/inventions/telegraph

History.com Editors. (2009o, November 9). *Napoleon Bonaparte.* History; A&E Television Networks. https://www.history.com/topics/european-history/napoleon

History.com Editors. (2009p, November 9). *Sir Francis Drake.* History; A&E Television Networks. https://www.history.com/topics/exploration/sir-francis-drake

History.com Editors. (2009q, November 12). *Seven Years' war.* History. https://www.history.com/topics/european-history/seven-years-war

History.com Editors. (2009r, November 16). *Benito Mussolini falls from power.* History. https://www.history.com/this-day-in-history/mussolini-falls-from-power

History.com Editors. (2009s, November 16). *German assault on Liege begins first battle of World War I.* History. https://www.history.com/this-day-in-history/german-assault-on-liege-begins-first-battle-of-world-war-i

History.com Editors. (2009t, December 2). *Leonidas.* History. https://www.history.com/topics/ancient-greece/leonidas

History.com Editors. (2009u, December 17). *Magna Carta.* History. https://www.history.com/topics/european-history/magna-carta

History.com Editors. (2010a, April 6). *California Gold Rush.* History. https://www.history.com/topics/19th-century/gold-rush-of-1849

History.com Editors. (2010b, April 16). *Cornelius Vanderbilt.* History; A&E Television Networks. https://www.history.com/topics/19th-century/cornelius-vanderbilt

History.com Editors. (2010c, April 22). *Middle Ages.* History; A&E Television Networks. https://www.history.com/topics/middle-ages/middle-ages

History.com Editors. (2010d, July 21). *Battle of Agincourt.* History. https://www.history.com/this-day-in-history/battle-of-agincourt

History.com Editors. (2010e, July 23). *Galileo Galilei.* History; A&E Television Networks. https://www.history.com/topics/inventions/galileo-galilei

History.com Editors. (2010f, July 30). *Mahatma Gandhi.* History. https://www.history.com/topics/asian-history/mahatma-gandhi

History.com Editors. (2010g, September 17). *Black Death.* History; A&E Television Networks. https://www.history.com/topics/middle-ages/black-death

History.com Editors. (2011, June 13). *Machu Picchu.* History; A&E Television Networks. https://www.history.com/topics/south-america/machu-picchu

History.com Editors. (2015, March 11). *Inca.* History; A&E Television Networks. https://www.history.com/topics/south-america/inca

History.com Editors. (2017a, August 10). *British Parliament.* History. https://www.history.com/topics/european-history/british-parliament

History.com Editors. (2017b, November 17). *Inquisition.* History. https://www.history.com/topics/religion/inquisition

History.com Editors. (2018a, January 25). *Dunkirk.* History; A&E Television Networks. https://www.history.com/topics/world-war-ii/dunkirk

History.com Editors. (2018b, February 2). *Parthenon.* History; A&E Television Networks. https://www.history.com/topics/ancient-greece/parthenon

History.com Editors. (2018c, April 4). *Renaissance.* History; A&E Television Networks. https://www.history.com/topics/renaissance/renaissance

History.com Editors. (2018d, April 5). *Huns.* History. https://www.history.com/topics/ancient-china/huns

History.com Editors. (2018e, August 21). *Abraham Lincoln elected president.* History. https://www.history.com/this-day-in-history/abraham-lincoln-elected-president

History.com Editors. (2018f, August 21). *Bartolomeu Dias.* History; A&E Television Networks. https://www.history.com/topics/exploration/bartolomeu-dias

History.com Editors. (2018g, August 21). *Delphi.* History. https://www.history.com/topics/ancient-greece/delphi

History.com Editors. (2018h, August 21). *Ellis Island.* History; A&E Television Networks. https://www.history.com/topics/immigration/ellis-island

History.com Editors. (2018i, August 21). *Ephesus*. History. https://www.history.com/topics/ancient-greece/ephesus

History.com Editors. (2018j, August 21). *Hernando de Soto*. History. https://www.history.com/topics/exploration/hernando-de-soto

History.com Editors. (2018k, August 21). *Juan Ponce de León*. History; A&E Television Networks. https://www.history.com/topics/exploration/juan-ponce-de-leon

History.com Editors. (2018l, August 21). *Kaiser Wilhelm II*. History. https://www.history.com/topics/world-war-i/kaiser-wilhelm-ii

History.com Editors. (2018m, August 21). *Machiavelli*. History; A&E Television Networks. https://www.history.com/topics/renaissance/machiavelli

History.com Editors. (2018n, August 21). *Nazca Lines*. History; A&E Television Networks. https://www.history.com/topics/south-america/nazca-lines

History.com Editors. (2018o, August 21). *Paris liberated*. History. https://www.history.com/this-day-in-history/paris-liberated

History.com Editors. (2018p, August 21). *Samurai and Bushido*. History. https://www.history.com/topics/asian-history/samurai-and-bushido

History.com Editors. (2018q, August 21). *Shang Dynasty*. History. https://www.history.com/topics/ancient-china/shang-dynasty

History.com Editors. (2018r, August 21). *Tang Dynasty*. History; A&E Television Networks. https://www.history.com/topics/ancient-china/tang-dynasty

History.com Editors. (2018s, August 21). *Third Battle of Ypres begins in Flanders*. History. https://www.history.com/this-day-in-history/third-battle-of-ypres-begins-in-flanders

History.com Editors. (2018t, August 21). *U.S. troops score victory at Cantigny*. History. https://www.history.com/this-day-in-history/u-s-troops-score-victory-at-cantigny

History.com Editors. (2018u, August 23). *Ancient Greek Democracy*. History; A&E Television Networks. https://www.history.com/topics/ancient-greece/ancient-greece-democracy

History.com Editors. (2018v, August 25). *September 11 attacks*. History; A&E Television Networks. https://www.history.com/topics/21st-century/9-11-attacks

History.com Editors. (2018w, August 29). *Maya*. History; A&E Television Networks. https://www.history.com/topics/ancient-americas/maya

History.com Editors. (2018x, September 12). *Francisco Pizarro*. History; A&E Television Networks. https://www.history.com/topics/exploration/francisco-pizarro

History.com Editors. (2018y, September 12). *Fugitive Slave Acts*. History; A&E Television Networks. https://www.history.com/topics/black-history/fugitive-slave-acts

History.com Editors. (2018z, September 12). *Henry Hudson*. History; A&E Television Networks. https://www.history.com/topics/exploration/henry-hudson

History.com Editors. (2018aa, September 12). *Marco Polo*. History; A&E Television Networks. https://www.history.com/topics/exploration/marco-polo

History.com Editors. (2018ab, September 13). *Battles of Lexington and Concord*. History; A&E Television Networks. https://www.history.com/topics/american-revolution/battles-of-lexington-and-concord

History.com Editors. (2018ac, September 20). *Ferdinand Magellan*. History; A&E Television Networks. https://www.history.com/topics/exploration/ferdinand-magellan

History.com Editors. (2018ad, October 2). *Byzantine Empire*. History. https://www.history.com/topics/ancient-middle-east/byzantine-empire

History.com Editors. (2019a, January 9). *William Shakespeare born*. History; A&E Television Networks. https://www.history.com/this-day-in-history/william-shakespeare-born

History.com Editors. (2019b, February 20). *Japan surrenders*. History; A&E Television Networks. https://www.history.com/this-day-in-history/japan-surrenders

History.com Editors. (2019c, February 20). *Rome founded*. History. https://www.history.com/this-day-in-history/rome-founded

History.com Editors. (2019d, February 22). *Congress enforces prohibition*. History. https://www.history.com/this-day-in-history/congress-enforces-prohibition

History.com Editors. (2019e, February 22). *Pope Urban II orders first Crusade*. History; A&E Television Networks. https://www.history.com/this-day-in-history/pope-urban-ii-orders-first-crusade

History.com Editors. (2019f, February 26). *Pizarro traps Incan emperor Atahualpa*. History; A&E Television Networks. https://www.history.com/this-day-in-history/pizarro-traps-incan-emperor-atahualpa

History.com Editors. (2019g, March 22). *China: Timeline*. History.com. https://www.history.com/topics/asian-history/china-timeline

History.com Editors. (2019h, April 4). *First modern Olympic Games*. History. https://www.history.com/this-day-in-history/first-modern-olympic-games

History.com Editors. (2019i, July 28). *Cook discovers Hawaii*. History. https://www.history.com/this-day-in-history/cook-discovers-hawaii

History.com Editors. (2019j, August 20). *Plymouth Colony*. History; A&E Television Networks. https://www.history.com/topics/colonial-america/plymouth

History.com Editors. (2019k, September 3). *Louisiana*. History. https://www.history.com/topics/us-states/louisiana

History.com Editors. (2019l, October 10). *Cotton Gin and Eli Whitney*. History; A&E Television Networks. https://www.history.com/topics/inventions/cotton-gin-and-eli-whitney

History.com Editors. (2019m, November 17). *Oliver Cromwell - definition, facts & head*. History. https://www.history.com/topics/european-history/oliver-cromwell

History.com Editors. (2021, October 12). *Rosie the Riveter*. History.com. https://www.history.com/topics/world-war-ii/rosie-the-riveter

History.com Editors. (2022a, October 4). *Joseph Stalin: Death, quotes & facts*. History; A&E Television Networks. https://www.history.com/topics/european-history/joseph-stalin

History.com Editors. (2022b, November 1). *Vladimir Lenin*. History; A&E Television Networks. https://www.history.com/topics/european-history/vladimir-lenin

History.com Editors. (2023, June 30). *Macedonia*. History.com. https://www.history.com/topics/ancient-greece/macedonia

History.com editors. (2009, October 27). *Civil Rights Movement*. History.com; A&E Television Networks. https://www.history.com/topics/black-history/civil-rights-movement

Hudson Museum. (2013, January 8). *Ballgame - Hudson Museum - University of Maine*. Hudson Museum. https://umaine.edu/hudsonmuseum/collections/william-p-palmer-iii/maya/ballgame-2/

Hudson, M. (2018). Fall of Constantinople | summary. In *Encyclopædia Britannica*. https://www.britannica.com/event/Fall-of-Constantinople-1453

Imperial War Museums. (n.d.). *18 minutes that shocked the world*. Imperial War Museums. https://www.iwm.org.uk/history/18-minutes-that-shocked-the-world

Imperial War Museums. (2000). *The 10 things you need to know about D-Day*. Imperial War Museums. https://www.iwm.org.uk/history/the-10-things-you-need-to-know-about-d-day

Imperial War Museums. (2018a). *8 things you need to know about the Battle of Britain*. Imperial War Museums. https://www.iwm.org.uk/history/8-things-you-need-to-know-about-the-battle-of-britain

Imperial War Museums. (2018b). *Who was Edith Cavell?* Imperial War Museums. https://www.iwm.org.uk/history/who-was-edith-cavell

JCU. (2019). *Who was John Cabot*. Johncabot.edu. https://www.johncabot.edu/about-jcu/who-was-john-cabot.aspx

Johns, K. (2023, May 12). *Sulla: The story of Rome's lucky dictator*. TheCollector. https://www.thecollector.com/lucius-cornelius-sulla-dictator/

Johnson, D. (2022, October 16). *Revolutionary PHL: Exiled from Philadelphia: Quakers during the Revolution*. American Philosophical Society. https://www.amphilsoc.org/blog/revolutionary-phl-exiled-philadelphia-quakers-during-revolution

Kale, S. (2021, June 8). *From chaturanga to chess- The history of the origin of chess*. Homegrown.co.in. https://homegrown.co.in/from-chaturanga-to-chess-the-history-of-the-origin-of-chess

Kapach, A. (2023, March 24). *Pegasus*. Mythopedia. https://mythopedia.com/topics/pegasus

Karnad, R. (2015, August 22). In WWII, millions of Indians fought for A Britain they abhorred. *NPR.org*. https://www.npr.org/2015/08/22/433515258/in-wwii-millions-of-indians-fought-for-a-britain-they-abhored

Kat Eschner. (2017, February 7). *A fanatical monk inspired 15th-century Italians to burn their clothes, makeup and art*. Smithsonian; Smithsonian.com. https://www.smithsonianmag.com/smart-news/when-fanatical-monk-took-over-florence-and-burned-bunch-vanities-180962005/

Kiger, P. J. (2018, November 8). *Why World War I ended with an armistice instead of a surrender*. History. https://www.history.com/news/world-war-i-armistice-germany-allies

Kiger, P. J. (2020, September 29). *How St. Augustine became the first European settlement in America*. History. https://www.history.com/news/st-augustine-first-american-settlement

Kiger, P. J. (2021a, April 28). *How World War I fueled the Russian Revolution*. History.com. https://www.history.com/news/world-war-i-russian-revolution

Kiger, P. J. (2021b, July 26). *8 facts about Ancient Egypt's hieroglyphic writing*. History. https://www.history.com/news/hieroglyphics-facts-ancient-egypt

Kiilleen, A. (2017, November 8). *Japan's victory in World War I*. U.S. Naval Institute. https://www.usni.org/magazines/naval-history-magazine/2021/june/japans-victory-world-war-i

Kim, D. (2002). *Martial Arts along the Silk Road: from Bodhidharma to Bruce Lee*. Smithsonian Folklife Festival. https://festival.si.edu/2002/the-silk-road/martial-arts-along-the-silk-road-from-bodhidharma-to-bruce-lee/smithsonian

Klein, C. (2018, August 23). *10 things you may not know about the Marquis de Lafayette*. History. https://www.history.com/news/10-things-you-may-not-know-about-the-marquis-de-lafayette

Kolipakam, V., Jordan, F. M., Dunn, M., Greenhill, S. J., Bouckaert, R., Gray, R. D., & Verkerk, A. (2018). A Bayesian phylogenetic study of the Dravidian language family. *Royal Society Open Science*, *5*(3), 171504. https://doi.org/10.1098/rsos.171504

Kosa, J., & Johnson, V. (2018, July 31). *The Powhatan Confederation*. Www.librarypoint.org. https://www.librarypoint.org/blogs/post/powhatan-confederation/

Kühner, H. (2020). Julius II | pope | Britannica. In *Encyclopædia Britannica*. https://www.britannica.com/biography/Julius-II

KY Historical Society. (n.d.). *The discovery of the Ohio River*. KY Historical Society. Retrieved September 20, 2023, from https://history.ky.gov/markers/the-discovery-of-the-ohio-river

Lal, R., Reicosky, D. C., & Hanson, J. D. (2007). Evolution of the plow over 10,000 years and the rationale for no-till farming. *Soil and Tillage Research*, *93*(1), 1–12. https://doi.org/10.1016/j.still.2006.11.004

Langston, L. S. (2022, February 3). *Gears drive the world*. American Scientist. https://www.americanscientist.org/article/gears-drive-the-world

Lanhers, Y., & Vale, M. (2023). Saint Joan of Arc | French heroine. In *Encyclopædia Britannica*. https://www.britannica.com/biography/Saint-Joan-of-Arc

Lesso, R. (2022, April 18). *What is the minotaur?* TheCollector. https://www.thecollector.com/what-is-the-minotaur/

Lewis, J. J. (2019a). *All about Empress Suiko of Japan, the first Japanese woman ruler*. ThoughtCo. https://www.thoughtco.com/empress-suiko-of-japan-biography-3528831

Lewis, J. J. (2019b). *Biography of Isabella d'Este, patron of the Renaissance*. ThoughtCo. https://www.thoughtco.com/isabella-deste-bio-3529705

Library of Congress. (n.d.-a). *Establishing the Georgia Colony, 1732-1750 | Colonial settlement, 1600s - 1763 | U.S. history primary source timeline | classroom materials at the Library of Congress*. Library of Congress, Washington, D.C. 20540 USA. https://www.loc.gov/classroom-materials/united-states-history-primary-source-timeline/colonial-settlement-1600-1763/georgia-colony-1732-1750/

Library of Congress. (n.d.-b). *Russian Discovery | Alaska* . Library of Congress, Washington, D.C. 20540 USA. https://www.loc.gov/collections/meeting-of-frontiers/articles-and-essays/alaska/russian-discovery/

Library of Congress. (n.d.-c). *The Zimmermann Telegram | For or against war | arguing over war | explore | echoes of the Great War: American experiences of World War I* . Library of Congress, Washington, D.C. 20540 USA. https://www.loc.gov/exhibitions/world-war-i-american-experiences/about-this-exhibition/arguing-over-war/for-or-against-war/the-zimmerman-telegram/

Library of Congress. (2015a). *History of the cylinder phonograph*. The Library of Congress. https://www.loc.gov/collections/edison-company-motion-pictures-and-sound-recordings/articles-and-essays/history-of-edison-sound-recordings/history-of-the-cylinder-phonograph/

Library of Congress. (2015b). *The Transcontinental Railroad | History of railroads and maps* . The Library of Congress. https://www.loc.gov/collections/railroad-maps-1828-to-1900/articles-and-essays/history-of-railroads-and-maps/the-transcontinental-railroad/

Library of Congress. (2022, March 16). *Indian Removal Act: Primary documents in American history*. Www.loc.gov. https://www.loc.gov/rr/program//bib/ourdocs/indian.html

Lienau, L. (2013, April 13). *A brief history of perspective*. Oklahoma Academy of Classical Art. https://www.classicalart.org/blog/a-brief-history-of-perspective

Lienhard, J. H. (n.d.-a). *Harington's john | The engines of our ingenuity*. Engines.egr.uh.edu. Retrieved September 19, 2023, from https://engines.egr.uh.edu/episode/846

Lienhard, J. H. (n.d.-b). *The first mechanical clocks | The engines of our ingenuity*. Engines.egr.uh.edu. https://engines.egr.uh.edu/episode/1506

Lira, C. (2001). *Savery pump*. Msu.edu. https://www.egr.msu.edu/~lira/supp/steam/savery.htm

Lo Iacono, V. (2020, January 24). *Bharathanatyam tradition classical Indian Dance and Bharata Natyam*. World Dance Heritage Research Centre. https://worlddanceheritage.org/bharathanatyam/

Lockett, C. J. (2022, May 31). *Ferdinand and Isabella: The marriage that unified Spain*. TheCollector. https://www.thecollector.com/marriage-of-ferdinand-and-isabella/

Lubow, A. (2007, November). *The gates of paradise*. Smithsonian Magazine. https://www.smithsonianmag.com/arts-culture/the-gates-of-paradise-174431341/

Lubow, A. (2009, July 1). *Terra Cotta Soldiers on the march*. Smithsonian; Smithsonian.com. https://www.smithsonianmag.com/history/terra-cotta-soldiers-on-the-march-30942673/

Lumen Learning. (2019). *The Eastern Zhou period | World Civilization*. Lumenlearning.com. https://courses.lumenlearning.com/suny-hccc-worldcivilization/chapter/the-eastern-zhou-period/

Lyons, J. (2011). *The house of wisdom*. Bloomsbury Publishing USA.

Machaca, M. (n.d.). *The Inca Trilogy - The condor, the puma, and the serpent | Kuoda Travel*. Kuoda Travel. https://www.kuodatravel.com/the-inca-trilogy/

Machicao, M. (2023, August 4). Lake Titicaca drying up as heat wave turns winter upside down. *Reuters*. https://www.reuters.com/world/americas/lake-titicaca-drying-up-heat-wave-turns-winter-upside-down-2023-08-04/

Maestri, N. (2019). *Historical evidence for Aztlan, the mythical Aztec homeland*. ThoughtCo. https://www.thoughtco.com/aztlan-the-mythical-homeland-169913

Makos, I. (2021, January 21). *Roles of Native Americans during the Revolution*. American Battlefield Trust. https://www.battlefields.org/learn/articles/roles-native-americans-during-revolution

Marshall, H. E. (1912). *A History of France*. https://www.heritage-history.com/index.php?c=read&author=marshall&book=france&story=_front

Mason, E. (2018, December 27). *10 things you (probably) didn't know about the Anglo-Saxons*. History Extra; History Extra. https://www.historyextra.com/period/anglo-saxon/facts-anglo-saxons-dates/

MasterClass. (2022, August 12). *Mercantilism history: How mercantile economic systems work*. Masterclass.com. https://www.masterclass.com/articles/mercantilism-history

Masur, G. S. (2019). Simon Bolivar. In *Encyclopædia Britannica*. https://www.britannica.com/biography/Simon-Bolivar

Mayan Civilization. (2019). Encyclopedia.com. https://www.encyclopedia.com/history/encyclopedias-almanacs-transcripts-and-maps/mayan-civilization

McHugh, J. (2020). *Andean Textiles*. Metmuseum.org. https://www.metmuseum.org/toah/hd/adtx/hd_adtx.htm

McLellan, D. T., & Chambre, H. (2018). Marxism | history, ideology, & examples. In *Encyclopædia Britannica*. https://www.britannica.com/topic/Marxism

McNeill, J. R. (2022). Columbian Exchange | diseases, animals, & plants. In *Encyclopedia Britannica*. https://www.britannica.com/event/Columbian-exchange

McWhorter, J. (2020, August 19). *Origin of language: When did it start and how did it evolve?* Wondrium Daily. https://www.wondriumdaily.com/origin-of-language-when-did-it-start-and-how-did-it-evolve/

Menon, A. (n.d.). *The Gupta period (article) | South Asia.* Khan Academy. https://www.khanacademy.org/humanities/art-asia/south-asia/x97ec695a:1000-b-c-e-500ce-indo-gangetic-plain/a/the-gupta-period

Metcalfe, T. (2023, July 21). *What was the Manhattan Project?* Scientific American. https://www.scientificamerican.com/article/what-was-the-manhattan-project/

Meyer, I. (2022, May 13). *Donatello "David" - looking at Donatello's two "David" sculptures.* Artincontext.org. https://artincontext.org/donatello-david/

Meyer, M. C., & Willey, G. R. (2018). Mexico - The rise of the Aztecs. In *Encyclopædia Britannica.* https://www.britannica.com/place/Mexico/The-rise-of-the-Aztecs

Michals, D. (2015). *Abigail Smith Adams.* National Women's History Museum. https://www.womenshistory.org/education-resources/biographies/abigail-adams

Milligan, M. (2022, July 25). *The real William Wallace – "Braveheart."* HeritageDaily - Archaeology News. https://www.heritagedaily.com/2022/07/the-real-william-wallace-braveheart/144192

Mills, E. (2023, January 1). *The flaming ships of Red Cliffs.* U.S. Naval Institute. https://www.usni.org/magazines/naval-history-magazine/2023/february/flaming-ships-red-cliffs

Ministry for Culture and Heritage. (2014a). *Ottoman Empire enters the First World War - The Ottoman Empire | NZHistory, New Zealand history online.* Govt.nz. https://nzhistory.govt.nz/war/ottoman-empire/enters-the-war

Ministry for Culture and Heritage. (2014b). *The Arab Revolt, 1916-18 - The Ottoman Empire.* Govt.nz. https://nzhistory.govt.nz/war/ottoman-empire/arab-revolt

Ministry of Antiquities. (2019). *Valley of the Kings.* Egymonuments.gov.eg. https://egymonuments.gov.eg/archaeological-sites/valley-of-the-kings/

Minster, C. (2020, August 27). *The mighty sun god of the Inca.* ThoughtCo. https://www.thoughtco.com/inti-the-inca-sun-god-2136316

Minster, C. (2023, April 5). *9 things you didn't know about Quetzalcoatl.* ThoughtCo. https://www.thoughtco.com/facts-about-quetzalcoatl-2136322

Mohammed, F. (2019, March 1). *Who was La Malinche? | JSTOR daily.* JSTOR Daily. https://daily.jstor.org/who-was-la-malinche/

Morgan Library and Museum. (2013, May 9). *The great experiment: George Washington and the American Republic.* The Morgan Library & Museum. https://www.themorgan.org/exhibitions/the-great-experiment

Morrill, J. S., & Greenblatt, S. J. (2018). Elizabeth I | Biography, Facts, Mother, & Death. In *Encyclopædia Britannica.* https://www.britannica.com/biography/Elizabeth-I

Mount Vernon Ladies' Association. (2019). *Revolutionary war battles.* George Washington's Mount Vernon; Mount Vernon. https://www.mountvernon.org/george-washington/the-revolutionary-war/washingtons-revolutionary-war-battles/

Mount Vernon Ladies Association. (2023). *Surveying.* George Washington's Mount Vernon. https://www.mountvernon.org/george-washington/washingtons-youth/surveying/

Myrstener, E., Lidberg, W., Segerström, U., Biester, H., Damell, D., & Bindler, R. (2016). Was Moshyttan the earliest iron blast furnace in Sweden? The sediment record as an archeological toolbox. *Journal of Archaeological Science: Reports, 5*, 35–44. https://doi.org/10.1016/j.jasrep.2015.10.040

Nanji, A., & Niyozov, S. (2019). *The Silk Road: Crossroads and encounters of faiths.* Smithsonian Folklife Festival. https://festival.si.edu/2002/the-silk-road/the-silk-road-crossroads-and-encounters-of-faith/smithsonian

NASA. (2007, November 23). *NASA - STS-1.* Www.nasa.gov. https://www.nasa.gov/mission_pages/shuttle/sts1/index.html

National Archives. (2018, October 16). *The Meuse-Argonne Offensive.* National Archives. https://www.archives.gov/research/military/ww1/meuse-argonne

National Archives. (2021, September 23). *Surrender of Germany (1945).* National Archives. https://www.archives.gov/milestone-documents/surrender-of-germany

National Gallery of Art. (2016, March 21). *Artist info.* Www.nga.gov. https://www.nga.gov/collection/artist-info.1342.html

National Geographic Society. (2020, May 20). *Kublai Khan.* Education.nationalgeographic.org. https://education.nationalgeographic.org/resource/kublai-khan/

National Geographic Society. (2022a, May 20). *Greek city-states | National Geographic Society.* Education.nationalgeographic.org. https://education.nationalgeographic.org/resource/greek-city-states/

National Geographic Society. (2022b, May 20). *Jainism | National Geographic Society.* Education.nationalgeographic.org. https://education.nationalgeographic.org/resource/jainism/

National Geographic Society. (2022c, May 20). *Jul 16, 1054 CE: Great Schism.* Education.nationalgeographic.org. https://education.nationalgeographic.org/resource/great-schism/

National Geographic Society. (2022d, May 20). *Mauryan Empire | National Geographic Society.* Education.nationalgeographic.org. https://education.nationalgeographic.org/resource/mauryan-empire/

National Geographic Society. (2022e, May 20). *The Peloponnesian War | National Geographic Society.* Education.nationalgeographic.org. https://education.nationalgeographic.org/resource/peloponnesian-war/

National Geographic Society. (2022f, May 20). *Three crowned kings of Tamilakam.* Education.nationalgeographic.org. https://education.nationalgeographic.org/resource/three-crowned-kings-tamilakam/

National Geographic Society. (2022g, June 2). *Seven Wonders of the Ancient World.* Education.nationalgeographic.org; National Geographic Society. https://education.nationalgeographic.org/resource/seven-wonders-ancient-world/

National Geographic Society. (2022h, September 28). *Mar 15, 44 BC: Julius Caesar assassinated | National Geographic Society.* Education.nationalgeographic.org; National Geographic. https://education.nationalgeographic.org/resource/julius-caesar-assassinated/

National Geographic Society. (2022i, September 28). *Roman Republic | National Geographic Society.* Education.nationalgeographic.org. https://education.nationalgeographic.org/resource/roman-republic/

National Geographic Society. (2022j, October 4). *Treaty of Tordesillas.* Education.nationalgeographic.org. https://education.nationalgeographic.org/resource/treaty-tordesillas/

National Geographic Society. (2022k, October 27). *The Art of War | National Geographic Society.* Education.nationalgeographic.org. https://education.nationalgeographic.org/resource/art-war/

National Geographic Society. (2022l, November 7). *Compass.* Education.nationalgeographic.org. https://education.nationalgeographic.org/resource/compass/

National Museum of American History. (2018, May 24). *Territory worth contesting.* National Museum of American History. https://americanhistory.si.edu/american-revolution/territory-worth-contesting

National Park Service. (2016). *Little Bighorn battlefield national monument (U.S. National Park Service).* Nps.gov. https://www.nps.gov/libi/index.htm

National Park Service. (2017). *Birth of a national park - Yellowstone National Park (U.S. National Park Service).* Nps.gov. https://www.nps.gov/yell/learn/historyculture/yellowstoneestablishment.htm

National Park Service. (2019). *Tecumseh.* Nps.gov. https://www.nps.gov/people/tecumseh.htm

National Park Service. (2020, October 15). *What is the Underground Railroad? - Underground Railroad (U.S. National Park Service).* Nps.gov. https://www.nps.gov/subjects/undergroundrailroad/what-is-the-underground-railroad.htm

Newman, T. (2006). *Tasmania, the name.* Www.utas.edu.au. https://www.utas.edu.au/library/companion_to_tasmanian_history/T/Tasmania%20name.htm

Nielbock, M. (2018, February 4). *Navigating with the kamal – Northern Hemisphere.* Astroedu.iau.org. https://astroedu.iau.org/en/activities/1647/navigating-with-the-kamal-northern-hemisphere/

NIH. (2020). *Mayans report smallpox spread to Yucatan Peninsula - Timeline - Native Voices.* Nih.gov. https://www.nlm.nih.gov/nativevoices/timeline/180.html

Nix, E. (2014, October 29). *Why is a marathon 26.2 miles?* History. https://www.history.com/news/why-is-a-marathon-26-2-miles

Nix, E. (2018, August 23). *What is the Rosetta Stone?* History. https://www.history.com/news/what-is-the-rosetta-stone

Nolan, H. (2019). *Anne Boleyn : 500 years of lies.* Little A.

NOVA. (2000). *NOVA Online | Secrets of lost empires | China bridge | Suspension bridge.* Www.pbs.org. https://www.pbs.org/wgbh/nova/lostempires/china/meetsusp.html

NPR. (2020). *Jeanne Baret.* Npr.org. https://www.npr.org/2010/12/26/132265308/a-female-explorer-discovered-on-the-high-seas

O'Connell, R. (2021, March 15). *The long lost city of Tamão is hiding in plain sight.* Travel. https://www.nationalgeographic.com/travel/article/long-lost-city-tamao-hiding-in-plain-sight

O'Connor, J. J., & Robertson, E. F. (2020). *Luca Pacioli - biography.* Maths History. https://mathshistory.st-andrews.ac.uk/Biographies/Pacioli/

Office of Energy Efficiency & Renewable Energy. (2013, November 22). *Internal combustion engine basics.* Energy.gov. https://www.energy.gov/eere/vehicles/articles/internal-combustion-engine-basics

Office of the Historian. (2019). *Milestones: 1776–1783 - Office of the Historian.* State.gov. https://history.state.gov/milestones/1776-1783/articles

Office of the Historian . (2019). *Milestones: 1914–1920 - Office of the Historian.* State.gov. https://history.state.gov/milestones/1914-1920/wwi

Oleinik, G. (2018, November 9). *The Greek hoplite.* Medium. https://gleboleinik.medium.com/the-greek-hoplite-543d2d25259d

Opera Magazine. (2020, December 16). *The Medici family and the Florence cathedral.* Duomo.firenze.it. https://duomo.firenze.it/en/opera-magazine/post/5231/the-medici-family-and-the-florence-cathedral

Other, A. N. (2014, September 23). *The shot that stopped Pfalz.* Naval Historical Society of Australia. https://navyhistory.au/the-shot-that-stopped-pfalz/

P.T. Limted. (2017, September 26). *History of weighing.* Medium. https://medium.com/@PTGlobal/history-of-weighing-f5b6874cfc11

Patton, J. (2022). *Gas in the Great War.* Www.kumc.edu; The University of Kansas. https://www.kumc.edu/school-of-medicine/academics/departments/history-and-philosophy-of-medicine/archives/wwi/essays/medicine/gas-in-the-great-war.html

PBS. (n.d.). *Africans in America/Part 1/Prince Henry the Navigator.* Www.pbs.org. https://www.pbs.org/wgbh/aia/part1/1p259.html

PBS. (2005). *Guns germs & steel: Variables. Llamas.* Www.pbs.org. https://www.pbs.org/gunsgermssteel/variables/llamas.html

PBS. (2008a). *Episode 3 | The story of India - Timeline | PBS.* Www.pbs.org. https://www.pbs.org/thestoryofindia/timeline/3/

PBS. (2008b). *Indus Valley | The story of India - Photo gallery | PBS.* Www.pbs.org. https://www.pbs.org/thestoryofindia/gallery/photos/3.html

PBS. (2009). *Episode 1 | The story of India - Timeline | PBS.* Pbs.org. https://www.pbs.org/thestoryofindia/timeline/1/

PBS. (2017). *Reconstruction Amendments | Slavery by another name | PBS.* Reconstruction Amendments | Slavery by Another Name Bento | PBS. https://www.pbs.org/tpt/slavery-by-another-name/themes/reconstruction-amendments/

PBS. (2019). *Africans in America/Part 1/The Middle Passage.* Pbs.org. https://www.pbs.org/wgbh/aia/part1/1p277.html

Penn Language Center. (2015). *Quechua.* Upenn.edu. https://plc.sas.upenn.edu/quechua

Pennock, C. D. (2022). A warlike culture? Religion and war in the Aztec world. *History and Anthropology*, 1–24. https://doi.org/10.1080/02757206.2022.2060215

Plumpton, J. (2010, January 20). *The study of history and the practice of politics.* International Churchill Society. https://winstonchurchill.org/resources/speeches/speeches-about-winston-churchill/the-study-of-history-and-the-practice-of-politics/

Polónia, A., & Oliveira, L. (2019). Shipbuilding in Portuguese overseas settlements, 1500–1700. *International Journal of Maritime History, 31*(3), 539–558. https://doi.org/10.1177/0843871419862711

Ponti, C. (2019, August 26). *America's history of slavery began long before Jamestown.* History. https://www.history.com/news/american-slavery-before-jamestown-1619

Potatoes USA. (n.d.). *Potato facts | Fun facts about potatoes.* Potatoes USA. https://potatogoodness.com/potato-fun-facts-history/

Powers, J. (1995). *Understanding Tibetan Buddhism - Bon - A heterodox System | Dreams of Tibet | FRONTLINE | PBS.* Www.pbs.org. https://www.pbs.org/wgbh/pages/frontline/shows/tibet/understand/bon.html

Pruitt, S. (2018, August 29). *Who was Boudica?* History. https://www.history.com/news/who-was-boudica

Pruitt, S. (2019, September 13). *When Hitler tried (and failed) to be an artist*. History. https://www.history.com/news/adolf-hitler-artist-paintings-vienna

Pruitt, S. (2021, June 29). *Who invented television?* History. https://www.history.com/news/who-invented-television

Qin, A. (2018, March 8). Qiu Jin, beheaded by imperial forces, was "China's Joan of Arc." *The New York Times*. https://www.nytimes.com/interactive/2018/obituaries/overlooked-qiu-jin.html

Ranjan, R. (2023, July 10). *16 Mahajanapadas - History, location, capital, socio-economic development [NCERT Notes on Ancient Indian History For UPSC]*. BYJUS. https://byjus.com/free-ias-prep/ancient-history-16-mahajanapadas/

Reilly, E. C. (n.d.). *Miguel de Cervantes - Publication of Don Quixote*. Encyclopedia Britannica. https://www.britannica.com/biography/Miguel-de-Cervantes/Publication-of-Don-Quixote

Rodeck, D. (2021, June 9). *What is blockchain?* Forbes Advisor. https://www.forbes.com/advisor/investing/cryptocurrency/what-is-blockchain/

Roos, D. (2019, August 28). *7 ways the printing press changed the world*. History; A&E Television Networks. https://www.history.com/news/printing-press-renaissance

Roos, D. (2020, December 15). *The real story of Montezuma, the last of the Aztec emperors*. HowStuffWorks. https://history.howstuffworks.com/history-vs-myth/montezuma.htm

Roos, D. (2021a, February 24). *How the Aztec Empire was forged through a triple alliance*. History. https://www.history.com/news/aztec-empire-triple-alliance

Roos, D. (2021b, November 11). *7 foods developed by Native Americans*. History. https://www.history.com/news/native-american-foods-crops

Rosenberg, M. (2023, May 5). *How the Russians renamed a city three times in a century*. ThoughtCo. https://www.thoughtco.com/when-was-st-petersburg-known-as-petrograd-and-leningrad-4072464

Royde-Smith, J. G. (2023, September 20). *World War I - The end of the German war*. Encyclopedia Britannica. https://www.britannica.com/event/World-War-I/The-end-of-the-German-war

Runnebaum, A. (2015, October 1). *The lost kingdom of Yamatai*. Japan Daily. https://japandaily.jp/the-lost-kingdom-of-yamatai-1943/

Saelee, M. (2023, September 14). *Research guides: Assassination of Archduke Franz Ferdinand: Topics in chronicling America: Search strategies & selected articles*. Guides.loc.gov. https://guides.loc.gov/chronicling-america-assassination-franz-ferdinand/selected-articles

Schmal, J. P. (2020, July 22). *The Náhuatl language of Mexico: From Aztlán to the present day*. Indigenous Mexico. https://indigenousmexico.org/state-of-mexico/the-nahuatl-language-of-mexico-from-aztlan-to-the-present-day/

Science Museum. (2018, October 19). *Ahoy! Alexander Graham Bell and the first telephone call*. Science Museum. https://www.sciencemuseum.org.uk/objects-and-stories/ahoy-alexander-graham-bell-and-first-telephone-call

Science Museum. (2019, October 11). *The age of plastic: From Parkesine to pollution*. Science Museum. https://www.sciencemuseum.org.uk/objects-and-stories/chemistry/age-plastic-parkesine-pollution

Science Museum. (2021, February 23). *How was penicillin developed?* Science Museum. https://www.sciencemuseum.org.uk/objects-and-stories/how-was-penicillin-developed

Science Reference Section, Library of Congress. (2022, February 22). *Who is credited with inventing the telephone?* Library of Congress, Washington, D.C. 20540 USA. https://www.loc.gov/everyday-mysteries/technology/item/who-is-credited-with-inventing-the-telephone/

ScienceDirect. (2014). *Vulcanization - an overview | ScienceDirect Topics*. Sciencedirect.com. https://www.sciencedirect.com/topics/materials-science/vulcanization

Sellars, J. (2002). *Aurelius, Marcus | Internet Encyclopedia of Philosophy*. Internet Encyclopedia of Philosophy. https://iep.utm.edu/marcus-aurelius/

Sennebogen, E. (2009, March 2). *How pottery works*. HowStuffWorks. https://home.howstuffworks.com/green-living/pottery1.htm

Sharp, T. (2019, April 9). *The first hot-air balloon flight*. Space.com; Space. https://www.space.com/16595-montgolfiers-first-balloon-flight.html

Silk-Road.com. (2018). *Silk history - Silk-Road.com.* Silk Road. http://www.silk-road.com/artl/silkhistory.shtml

Simon, M. (2014, July 9). *Fantastically wrong: Why the Egyptians worshiped beetles that eat poop for a living.* Wired. https://www.wired.com/2014/07/fantastically-wrong-dung-beetle-worship/

Smithsonian Institute. (n.d.-a). The Legend of the Dwarf and the Governor. In *National Museum of the American Indian.* Retrieved September 12, 2023, from https://maya.nmai.si.edu/sites/default/files/resources/The%20Legend%20of%20the%20Dwarf%20and%20the%20Governor%20of%20Uxmal.pdf

Smithsonian Institute. (n.d.-b). *The origin of the metric system.* Smithsonian Institution. https://www.si.edu/spotlight/metric-system-demonstration-apparatus/the-origin-of-the-metric-system

Smithsonian Institute. (n.d.-c). *The safety bicycle and beyond.* Smithsonian Institution. https://www.si.edu/spotlight/si-bikes/si-bikes-safety

Smithsonian Institute. (2009, December 22). *Stone tools.* The Smithsonian Institution's Human Origins Program. https://humanorigins.si.edu/evidence/behavior/stone-tools

Smithsonian Institute. (2014). *The Four Suyus | Engineering the Inka Empire.* Si.edu. https://americanindian.si.edu/inkaroad/engineering/activity/four-suyus.html

Smithsonian's National Zoo. (2018, June 26). *American bison.* Smithsonian's National Zoo. https://nationalzoo.si.edu/animals/american-bison

Snell, M. (2020a, August 26). *Biography of Clovis, founder of the Merovingian dynasty.* ThoughtCo. https://www.thoughtco.com/profile-of-clovis-1788678

Snell, M. (2020b, August 27). *Avignon Papacy - When the popes resided in France.* ThoughtCo. https://www.thoughtco.com/the-avignon-papacy-1789454

Snell, M. (2021, September 23). *The Hospitallers - monastic knights.* ThoughtCo. https://www.thoughtco.com/the-knights-hospitaller-1788970

Solly, M. (2018, November 8). *The true story of Robert the Bruce, Scotland's "Outlaw King."* Smithsonian Magazine. https://www.smithsonianmag.com/history/true-story-robert-bruce-scotlands-outlaw-king-180970756/

Solly, M. (2020, March 12). *The myth of "Bloody Mary."* Smithsonian Magazine. https://www.smithsonianmag.com/history/myth-bloody-mary-180974221/

Solly, M. (2022, September 9). *The many myths of Catherine de' Medici.* Smithsonian Magazine. https://www.smithsonianmag.com/history/the-many-myths-of-catherine-de-medici-180980722/

Sorabella, J. (2019). *Monasticism in Western Medieval Europe.* Metmuseum.org. https://www.metmuseum.org/toah/hd/mona/hd_mona.htm

Spencer, E. H. (n.d.). *Research guides: Women in the French Revolution: A resource guide: Charlotte Corday.* Guides.loc.gov. https://guides.loc.gov/women-in-the-french-revolution/charlotte-corday

Spray, A. (2023, March 22). *What we know about Aguada Fénix: The oldest Mayan city ever discovered.* TheTravel. https://www.thetravel.com/what-to-know-about-the-maya-structure-of-aguada-fenix/

Sri Aurobindo Ashram. (n.d.). *Sri Aurobindo.* Www.sriaurobindoashram.org. https://www.sriaurobindoashram.org/sriaurobindo/

Staats, B. V. (2014, May 17). *English historical fiction authors: "...Till death us depart" -- Archbishop Cranmer's beloved, joan and margarete.* English Historical Fiction Authors. https://englishhistoryauthors.blogspot.com/2014/05/till-death-us-depart-archbishop.html

Standiford, L. (2010). *Meet you in hell: Andrew Carnegie, Henry Clay Frick, and the bitter partnership that transformed America.* Paw Prints.

Starke, H. D. (2019). Rosa Luxemburg. In *Encyclopædia Britannica.* https://www.britannica.com/biography/Rosa-Luxemburg

Stewart, J. (2012, June 14). *The button: A visual history of the world's sexiest fastening.* Slate Magazine. https://www.slate.com/articles/life/design/2012/06/button_history_a_visual_tour_of_button_design_through_the_ages_.html

Sundar, S. (2023, January 14). *If you still aren't sure what ChatGPT is, this is your guide to the viral chatbot that everyone is talking about.* Business Insider. https://www.businessinsider.com/everything-you-need-to-know-about-chat-gpt-2023-1

Swetz, F. J. (2008). *The Quipu.* https://doi.org/10.4169/loci003206

Szoblik, K. (2020). Traces of Aztec cultural memory in sixteenth-century songs and chronicles: The case of Tlacahuepan. *The Americas*, *77*(4), 513–537. https://doi.org/10.1017/tam.2020.35

Szymanski, T. (2004, May 4). *Papyrus making 101: An introduction to papyrus.* Apps.lib.umich.edu. https://apps.lib.umich.edu/papyrus_making/pm_intro.html

Taronas, L. (2023, February 11). *Akhenaten: The mysteries of religious revolution.* ARCE. https://arce.org/resource/akhenaten-mysteries-religious-revolution/

Tharoor, S. (2023, May 24). *Why India today shouldn't forget the legacy of Ambedkar.* Time. https://time.com/6282089/india-today-legacy-ambedkar/

The Getty Museum. (n.d.-a). *Aphrodite and the gods of love: Roman Venus (Getty Villa Exhibitions).* Www.getty.edu. https://www.getty.edu/art/exhibitions/aphrodite/venus.html#:~:text=Julius%20Caesar%20and%20his%20heir

The Getty Museum. (n.d.-b). *Chivalry in the Middle Ages (Getty Center Exhibitions).* Www.getty.edu. https://www.getty.edu/art/exhibitions/chivalry/

The Gilder Lehrman Institute of American History. (n.d.). *The Doctrine of Discovery, 1493.* Www.gilderlehrman.org. https://www.gilderlehrman.org/history-resources/spotlight-primary-source/doctrine-discovery-1493

The Holocaust Explained. (n.d.). *Strength and weaknesses of the Weimar Republic – The Holocaust Explained: Designed for schools.* The Wiener Holocaust Library. https://www.theholocaustexplained.org/the-nazi-rise-to-power/the-weimar-republic/strength-and-weaknesses-of-the-weimar-republic/

The Met. (2020). *Canopic jar.* Metmuseum.org. https://www.metmuseum.org/art/collection/search/550773

The National Archives. (2015, December 15). *The National Archives - Togoland and the first World War.* The National Archives Blog. https://blog.nationalarchives.gov.uk/togoland-first-world-war/

The National WWII Museum. (2023). *The Nuremberg Trials.* The National WWII Museum | New Orleans; The National WWII Museum. https://www.nationalww2museum.org/war/topics/nuremberg-trials

The Nobel Prize. (2018). *The Nobel Peace Prize 1964.* NobelPrize.org. https://www.nobelprize.org/prizes/peace/1964/king/biographical/

The Ohio State University. (2019). *Eleanor of Aquitaine | eHistory.* Osu.edu. https://ehistory.osu.edu/biographies/eleanor-aquitaine

The Wiener Holocaust Library. (n.d.). *The early years of the Nazi Party – The Holocaust explained: Designed for schools.* Theholocaustexplained.org. https://www.theholocaustexplained.org/the-nazi-rise-to-power/the-early-years-of-the-nazi-party/

theCollector. (2022, February 10). *What were the best inventions of the Renaissance? (Top 5).* TheCollector. https://www.thecollector.com/best-renaissance-inventions/

Theutenberg, B. J. (1984). Mare Clausum et Mare Liberum. *Arctic*, *37*(4), 481–492. https://www.jstor.org/stable/40510310

Tiwari, S. (2023). *Rigveda | Vedic Heritage Portal.* Vedicheritage.gov.in. https://vedicheritage.gov.in/samhitas/rigveda/

Torrent, D. (2012, September 14). *Earliest use of Mexican turkeys by ancient Maya.* Florida Museum. https://www.floridamuseum.ufl.edu/science/earliest-use-of-mexican-turkeys-by-ancient-maya/

Trachtman, P. (2002, March 1). *The secrets of Easter Island.* Smithsonian; Smithsonian.com. https://www.smithsonianmag.com/history/the-secrets-of-easter-island-59989046/

Tretkoff, E. (2019). *December 1938: Lise Meitner & Otto Frisch discover nuclear fission.* @Apsphysics. https://www.aps.org/publications/apsnews/200712/physicshistory.cfm

Trinity College Dublin. (2021, August 18). *The Book of Kells - The Library of Trinity College Dublin - Trinity College Dublin.* Www.tcd.ie. https://www.tcd.ie/library/research-collections/book-of-kells.php

Tuyuc, L. (2022, July 26). *The deliberately misguided Maya legacy.* The Indigenous Foundation. https://www.theindigenousfoundation.org/articles/addressing-the-deliberately-misguided-maya-legacy

UNC Libraries. (2012). *Mayan languages · Ancient and living Maya in the 19th and 20th centuries: archaeological discovery, literary voice, and political struggle · UNC Libraries.* Unc.edu. https://exhibits.lib.unc.edu/exhibits/show/maya/languages

UNESCO. (2019). *Venice | SILK ROADS.* Unesco.org. https://en.unesco.org/silkroad/content/venice

UNESCO World Heritage Centre. (n.d.). *Historic monuments of ancient Nara.* UNESCO World Heritage Centre. https://whc.unesco.org/en/list/870/

United Nations. (n.d.). *History of the United Nations*. United Nations. https://www.un.org/en/model-united-nations/history-united-nations

University of Florida. (2011). *UF study of lice DNA shows humans first wore clothes 170,000 years ago - News - University of Florida*. Ufl.edu. https://news.ufl.edu/archive/2011/01/uf-study-of-lice-dna-shows-humans-first-wore-clothes-170000-years-ago.html

University of Minnesota. (2016, March 22). *4.2 history of newspapers*. Umn.edu; University of Minnesota Libraries Publishing edition, 2016. This edition adapted from a work originally produced in 2010 by a publisher who has requested that it not receive attribution. https://open.lib.umn.edu/mediaandculture/chapter/4-2-history-of-newspapers/

University of Pittsburgh. (n.d.). *Yamato Period (250 – 710) | Japan Module*. Www.japanpitt.pitt.edu. https://www.japanpitt.pitt.edu/timeline/yamato-period-250-710

UNRV. (2019). *Gladiators in Ancient Rome | UNRV.com*. Unrv.com. https://www.unrv.com/entertainment/gladiators.php

ushistory.org. (2019). *Economic growth and the early Industrial Revolution*. Ushistory.org. https://www.ushistory.org/Us/22a.asp

Van Norden, B. (2019, September 6). *Mencius (Stanford Encyclopedia of Philosophy)*. Stanford.edu. https://plato.stanford.edu/entries/mencius/

Vasiloudis, D. (2022, September 4). *The history of writing; tracing the development of expressing language by systems of markings*. The Archaeologist. https://www.thearchaeologist.org/blog/the-history-of-writing-tracing-the-development-of-expressing-language-by-systems-of-markings

Vergun, D. (2020, January 8). *U.S. forces began main battle for Philippines 75 years ago*. U.S. Department of Defense. https://www.defense.gov/News/Feature-Stories/story/Article/2048611/us-forces-began-main-battle-for-philippines-75-years-ago/

Watson, R. A. (2019). Rene Descartes. In *Encyclopædia Britannica*. https://www.britannica.com/biography/Rene-Descartes

Watson, R. E. (2017). *The diet and subsistence methods of the Maya: Their health and cultural consequences fr al consequences from the Pre-Classic era to today* [Honors Thesis]. https://fisherpub.sjf.edu/cgi/viewcontent.cgi?article=1001&context=honors_undergrad

Watt, A. (2019, January 25). *These are the 10 most spectacular space missions in history*. Popular Mechanics. https://www.popularmechanics.com/space/g25941053/famous-space-missions-through-history/

Welford, J. (2022, June 28). *Manco Capac: Legendary founder of the Incas*. Medium. https://medium.com/@johnwelford15/manco-capac-legendary-founder-of-the-incas-779bc4a09797

Wellesley Art Department. (2017). *Origins of the temple · Temple of Jupiter Optimus Maximus · Piranesi in Rome*. Omeka.wellesley.edu. http://omeka.wellesley.edu/piranesi-rome/exhibits/show/temple-to-jupiter-optimus-maxi/origins-of-the-temple

West, D. (2019, November 27). *How did the Ancient Mayans discover aero?* Medium. https://medium.com/swlh/how-did-the-ancient-mayans-discover-zero-b74e637d9920

White, A. (2022, March 11). *The Mexican revolutionary who fought for freedom on the battlefield and in the barroom*. Atlas Obscura. https://www.atlasobscura.com/articles/petra-herrera-mexican-revoultion-spy

Wickramasinghe, C. S. M. (2021). The Indian invasion of Alexander and the emergence of hybrid cultures. *Indian Historical Review*, *48*(1), 69–91. https://doi.org/10.1177/03769836211009651

Wilde, R. (2019a). *Biography of Vlad the Impaler, inspiration for Dracula*. ThoughtCo. https://www.thoughtco.com/a-biography-of-vlad-the-impaler-vlad-iii-dracula-1221266

Wilde, R. (2019b). *History of Yugoslavia - Overview*. ThoughtCo. https://www.thoughtco.com/yugoslavia-1221863

Wilde, R. (2020, August 28). *Learn about the famous forgery, the Donation of Constantine*. ThoughtCo. https://www.thoughtco.com/the-donation-of-constantine-1221782

Wilde, R. (2023, April 26). *A guide to the intellectual movement known as renaissance humanism*. ThoughtCo. https://www.thoughtco.com/renaissance-humanism-p2-1221781

Wilke, C. (2021, November 24). *A brief scientific history of glass*. Smithsonian Magazine. https://www.smithsonianmag.com/science-nature/a-brief-scientific-history-of-glass-180979117/

Wilkinson, F. (2022, June 2). *The Protestant Reformation*. Education.nationalgeographic.org; National Geographic. https://education.nationalgeographic.org/resource/protestant-reformation/

Willis, K. (2021, August 30). *How Toussaint Louverture rose from slavery to lead the Haitian Revolution*. History.COM. https://www.history.com/news/toussaint-louverture-haiti-revolution

Winter, J. (2019, September 6). Robert Mugabe: From liberator to tyrant. *BBC News*. https://www.bbc.com/news/world-africa-27519044

Wisse, J. (2019). *Pieter Bruegel the Elder*. Metmuseum.org. https://www.metmuseum.org/toah/hd/brue/hd_brue.htm

Yee, L. K. (n.d.). *Chinese historical & cultural project - Teas wonderful history*. Chcp.org. https://chcp.org/teas-wonderful-history/

Yucatan Times. (2021, July 13). *On a day like today, the last Maya codex was burned by a Catholic priest in Yucatan*. The Yucatan Times. https://www.theyucatantimes.com/2021/07/on-a-day-like-today-the-last-maya-codex-was-burned-by-a-catholic-priest-in-yucatan/

Yucatan Today. (2014, June 11). *La Ceiba: Sacred Maya tree - Yucatan Today*. Yucatantoday.com. https://yucatantoday.com/en/la-ceiba-sacred-mayan-tree/

Yuko, E. (2021, August 17). *How cats became divine symbols in Ancient Egypt*. History. https://www.history.com/news/cats-ancient-egypt

Printed in Great Britain
by Amazon

35172132R00106